If you're caring for a lov
cognitive changes, *Beyond*
walk alongside you. This dis
faith-based inspiration and p

Whether facing communic ...hallenges or searching for moments of peace in your demanding day, these pages provide support and spiritual comfort. Each chapter addresses the unique complexities of your caregiving role, offering valuable guidance and understanding as you navigate this path.

Each chapter opens with a scripture and devotional that aligns with the corresponding chapter in *Beyond Memory's Veil: A Devotional for Those Experiencing Cognitive Changes.* This intentional pairing allows you both to reflect on the same spiritual message, creating opportunities for meaningful connection even as your journeys differ. While your loved one explores their experience through their book, you'll find parallel insights and guidance specifically tailored to your caregiving role.

Beyond Memory's Veil
Care Partner's Guide

Joyce Kostakis

Edition date: February 8, 2025
The scriptures are from the King James Version (KJV)
ISBN:
Print Copy: 978-1-7346673-8-7

A note from the author

I have created two devotional guides to assist you as a care partner and to help your loved one feel empowered as you both navigate the changes you are facing.

These devotionals work together while meeting each person's distinct needs. Though the daily readings are different, they share common themes that create meaningful opportunities for connection.

The care partner devotional offers support that focuses on your day-to-day experience, with encouraging words and practical steps to help you navigate challenges and grow stronger. For your loved one, their devotional brings hope and encouragement focused on their specific situation, helping them feel understood and empowered each day.

This personalized approach ensures each of you receive the support that will be most helpful during this time. The alignment of themes across the guides strengthens the partnership and mutual understanding between you.

I hope these devotionals provide a warm, supportive framework. These guides are here to sustain and strengthen each of you.

Each guide comes from my heart as a source of comfort and guidance. While I've worked to make everything as helpful and accurate, please remember the devotionals are offered as a source of spiritual encouragement and comfort.

While written with care and compassion:

- The devotionals are a spiritual comfort resource, not medical advice
- Always consult your loved one's healthcare team for medical decisions
- Each care partner's journey is unique, just as each person with dementia is unique
- Continue following all care plans and medical appointments for your loved one
- Take care of your own health and well-being too

For medical guidance, please rely on your healthcare professionals. For emotional support, don't hesitate to reach out to counselors, support groups, or other caregivers walking this path.

Dedication

Carole Klingler, founder of Dementia Friendly Life (LIFE) inspired this collection of scriptures, devotions, and tips. Carole's tireless work and her struggle to find faith-based resources prompted this book's creation.

LIFE is an invaluable organization that offers a variety of stimulating programs to aid individuals experiencing cognitive decline and the loved ones caring for them. These programs include art, music, and pet therapies, exercise sessions, care partner peer support, and lunch. Importantly, both the caregiver and their loved one attend the support group together, fostering a sense of community and mutual support.

There is no cost to participants or care partners. Participants, care partners, and supporters report feeling as though they are members of a family. For those seeking support in Northeast Ohio, LIFE currently offers programs in Amherst, Avon Lake, Elyria, North Ridgeville, Orrville, Wellington, and Wooster.

LIFE: A Dementia Friendly Foundation
P.O. Box 117
Oberlin, OH 44074
Tel.: 440-935-3506
Email: info@dflife.org
Facebook: www.facebook.com/dflife.org
Website: dflife.org

Memory Cafés were created as a comfortable space to socialize, listen to music, play games, and enjoy other activities. Imagine a gathering place where those with memory loss feel no shame or judgment, where they can laugh freely and rev up happy memories, where they can enjoy a renewed sense of vitality through exercise, dancing, playing games, or cuddling up to an adorable service dog.

TABLE OF CONTENTS

FOUNDATIONS OF CARE

Chapter 1: Embracing Support

Scripture: "Bear ye one another's burdens, and so fulfill the law of Christ." (Galatians 6:2, KJV)

As you start this chapter, know that your loved one can explore similar themes in their companion guide. Their first chapter helps show them how to maintain dignity and choice while accepting help, while your first chapter is about welcoming support that will sustain you both. Together, you're building a partnership grounded in mutual respect and understanding.

Devotional: In taking care of a loved one, one of your greatest challenges may not be managing daily tasks or appointments—it might be opening yourself to receive the support others want to give. God's design for community includes giving and receiving, creating connections that strengthen us all.

A close friend of mine shared something that really changed the way I saw accepting help. I admitted to her I struggled with letting others assist me and, on the rare times I did, I always felt like I needed to pay them back right away. She pointed out that giving and receiving aren't about keeping tabs.

Instead, she encouraged me to think about how good it feels to help someone else—that joy and fulfillment that comes from knowing you've made a difference. Then she said something that really stuck with me: When I turn down help, I'm robbing the other person of the chance to experience that feeling too.

That perspective was a game-changer. I realized that letting others help me doesn't burden them, but is actually a way to take part in the loving community God wants for us. When I accept what others offer, I'm honoring the give-and-take He intends for our relationships.

Prayer: *God, help me recognize and accept the support You provide through others. When I hesitate to receive help, remind me You created us to need one another. Thank You for those You've placed in my life to share this journey. Give me wisdom to receive support with grace, knowing it strengthens our entire community. Amen.*

The recent shift from "caregiver" to "care partner" reflects an important evolution in how we view this relationship. You might wonder, "Why does this matter? Aren't they just words?" But this change signifies an important evolution in perspective.

The term "care partner" repositions the caregiver and the person receiving care as collaborators rather than one person solely providing for the other. It creates a reciprocal relationship where both parties contribute and benefit, even if in different ways.

This change in wording helps us see the real value and dignity of the person being cared for. The term "care partner" emphasizes their active role in their care, rather than viewing them as passive recipients. This proves they still have a lot to contribute.

A partnership approach to caregiving can change the way we approach caregiving. Instead of a potentially burdensome, one-sided dynamic, we now have a collaborative journey of mutual support and growth. When we view ourselves as care partners, we foster deeper understanding, respect, and appreciation in our relationships.

While "caregiver" isn't wrong, it might make it sound like you have all the responsibility. Care partner is a gentle reminder we're all in this together - you, your family, friends, doctors, and even community services. Success depends on teamwork, where everyone, including you, has an important role to play.

Think of caregiving as a shared journey where you can and should draw upon multiple sources of support:

Your Support Network Includes:

1. Professional Resources:

- Healthcare providers offering medical guidance
- Social workers connecting you with services
- Respite care providers giving you needed breaks
- Counselors specializing in care partner support
- Adult day programs providing structured activities

2. Community Support:

- Local support groups sharing experiences
- Faith communities offering spiritual and practical help
- Neighbors willing to assist with everyday tasks
- Senior centers providing activities and connections

3. Family Involvement:

- Regular family meetings for care decisions

- Shared responsibility schedules
- Clear communication systems
- Planned respite coverage

Your loved one can remain actively involved in their own care. Even with changing abilities, they can express preferences, make choices, and participate in life decisions. Your job is to help and encourage them, not to control everything.

This partnership includes more than just you and your loved one. This is about creating a mutual support network for each of you. Care partners can include family, friends, support groups, respite care services, and healthcare providers. Don't be afraid to ask others for help.

The "care partner" mindset emphasizes that while you're a key player, it's important to remember that you're not expected—or meant—to do everything on your own. Adopting this approach helps you avoid burnout and stress, ultimately leading to better care for both your loved one and yourself. You might feel that no one can care for your loved one as well as you can, or that asking for help will burden others. Getting support from others doesn't reduce your importance or the special relationship you and your loved one have. Instead, it enhances the care you provide by bringing in fresh perspectives and allowing you moments of respite. Self-care is vital for effective caregiving.

Each person brings something valuable to the care partnership. The primary care partner brings their love and dedication. Others might bring specialized knowledge, a fresh perspective, or simply a friendly face and a listening ear.

By being open to this wider circle of support, you're enriching both of your lives with additional resources and relationships. This approach can help prevent burnout, reduce stress, and ensure a more comprehensive and sustainable care experience.

Embracing support is about extending an invitation for others to contribute their gifts and strengths. When you allow others to contribute their time, skills, and emotional support, you're creating a powerful network of care that uplifts everyone involved.

It's a win-win for everyone. One of the most significant benefits of accepting help is the opportunity for self-care. You may have heard the phrase "you can't pour from an empty cup." Taking care of yourself isn't selfish; it's necessary for providing consistent, quality care. By filling your cup or putting your life jacket on first, as another analogy goes, you can ensure you are there for your loved one.

It's normal to get overwhelmed, isolated, or even resentful. Acknowledge these feelings with compassion. When you get caught up in the stress and challenges of caregiving, pause and ground yourself in the present. Take a few deep breaths, notice your surroundings, and remind yourself of the love and dedication that motivates your care partnering.

Challenge: Feeling like you have to do everything on your own and resisting asking for help.

Solution: Embrace the care partner mindset and recognize that it's okay (and necessary) to reach out for support. Make a list of specific tasks you could use help with and start reaching out to family, friends, or community services.

Example: You've been struggling to keep up with your loved one's doctor appointments and your own work schedule. Ask a family member or friend if they can handle the next appointment or see if your neighbor can check in on your loved one occasionally while you're at the office.

Tips for Embracing Support:

1. Start by making a list of tasks or activities that others can assist with. This could include errands, meal preparation, household chores, or spending quality time with your loved one. Be specific and clear about what help you need and don't be afraid to ask. People often want to help but may not know how.

2. Communicate openly and honestly with your support network about your needs and boundaries. Let them know what you're comfortable with and what you prefer to handle yourself. This helps ensure that the help you receive aligns with your values and preferences, and prevents misunderstandings or overstepping.

3. Consider setting up a regular schedule for accepting help, such as having a friend or family member visit on certain days of the week. This predictability can provide a sense of structure

and reliability for you and your loved one, making it easier for others to plan their involvement.

4. Be open to different forms of help, such as emotional support, respite care, or help with paperwork and decision-making. Sometimes, the most valuable assistance may not be hands-on caregiving tasks, but rather the opportunity to share your experiences, get advice, or take a break.

5. Embrace technology as a tool for accepting help. There are many apps and online platforms that can help you coordinate care tasks, communicate with your support network, and access resources and information. Don't be afraid to explore these options and find what works best.

6. Express gratitude and appreciation for the help you receive. A simple "thank you" can go a long way in acknowledging the efforts of others and encouraging their continued support. Consider writing a thank-you note or finding other ways to show your appreciation.

7. Prioritize self-care and make time for activities that recharge and rejuvenate you. Accepting help from others can create space for you to engage in hobbies, spend time with friends, or simply rest and relax.

8. Seek out support groups or counseling services to connect with others who understand your experiences and can offer guidance and

encouragement. Opening up with others who "get it" can be incredibly validating and empowering, helping you feel less alone in your role as a care partner. Reach out for professional support when needed.

9. Shift your language and mindset from "caregiver" to "care partner" to emphasize collaboration and shared responsibility. This simple change can help you feel more supported and empowered in your role, reminding you that you're part of a team rather than carrying the entire burden alone.

10. Recognize and honor your loved one's dignity by involving them in decision-making as much as possible. Even as their abilities change, find ways to offer choices and respect their preferences. This collaborative approach can help maintain their sense of independence and strengthen your partnership in care.

It can feel like you're alone sometimes, especially on those tough days when everything seems to be going sideways. But there's an entire community facing similar challenges and sharing similar joys rooting for each other. Embrace this support. It's through our connections that you can find strength, wisdom, and the courage to face each new day with love and compassion.

Chapter 2: Building Your Support Network

Scripture: "Two are better than one; because they have a good reward for their labour." (Ecclesiastes 4:9, KJV)

Building on the care partnership foundation discussed in Chapter 1, this chapter explores how to develop and maintain a robust support network that benefits you and your loved one.

Devotional: In the journey of caregiving, God provides companions who strengthen and support us along the way. Through His wisdom, we learn that shared care multiplies blessings rather than dividing them. He gives us opportunities to build networks of support that reflect His vision of a loving community. When you build relationships with others, you create channels for His love to flow more abundantly.

Prayer: *God, guide me as I build connections that strengthen my caregiving journey. When I feel isolated, help me reach out to the community You've provided. Grant me wisdom to recognize and welcome the support You send through others. When I feel overwhelmed, remind me of the strength found in fellowship. Lead me to relationships that refresh and encourage my spirit. Amen.*

Challenge: Feeling overwhelmed by caregiving responsibilities and guilty about taking time for your own support needs.

Solution: Remember that caring for yourself is not selfish—it's essential. Your loved one benefits when you're well-supported and refreshed.

Example: You've been hesitant to attend a care partner support group, thinking you should spend that time with your loved one. Consider starting with just one meeting a month. Arrange for a respite care worker or family member to stay with your loved one during this time. You'll gain valuable strategies and emotional support that make you a more patient and effective care partner.

Practical Tips for Building Your Network:

1. Start Small

- Choose one support group to attend
- Connect with one other care partner
- Accept one offer of help this week
- Schedule one self-care activity

2. Use Technology Wisely

- Join online support communities
- Use care-coordination apps
- Set up video calls with distant family
- Try grocery delivery services

3. Create Care Teams

- List potential helpers and their strengths
- Assign specific tasks to willing helpers
- Use shared calendars for coordination
- Establish backup plans

4. Maintain Boundaries

- Set realistic expectations
- Communicate your needs clearly
- Schedule regular breaks
- Protect your personal time

5. Stay Connected

- Keep regular appointments with friends
- Maintain your own interests
- Schedule check-ins with supporters
- Join care partner education workshops

Remember:

- Strong support networks benefit you and your loved one
- Regular respite strengthens your ability to provide care
- Each person in your network brings unique gifts
- Building connections takes time and patience
- Your well-being directly impacts care quality

Nurturing your support network isn't just about getting help—it's about creating a community that enriches your life and your loved one's journey. Each connection you make, each resource you discover, adds strength and resilience to your care partnership.

Chapter 3: Understanding the Stages

Scripture: "To every thing there is a season, and a time to every purpose under the heaven." (Ecclesiastes 3:1, KJV)

As your loved one progresses through different stages, you're learning to understand and adapt to each phase. While these changes may feel overwhelming and unpredictable at first, God provides the discernment needed to respond with knowledge and tenderness. Through His grace, we find strength to adjust our care as needs change, treasuring each moment while preparing for tomorrow.

For day-to-day strategies in managing behavioral changes, see Chapter 27. For guidance on responding with compassion and spiritual strength, refer to Chapter 31.

Devotional: God's wisdom teaches us that every season has its purpose, even the difficult ones. As we witness changes in our loved ones, He reminds us that His presence remains constant through every transition. Through His grace, we learn that while abilities may shift, His love never changes. He guides our hearts to notice subtle changes and adapt our care, helping us treasure each moment while preparing for tomorrow. Just as He ordained the seasons to follow their natural progression, He walks alongside us through every stage of this journey, providing strength, wisdom, and understanding exactly when we need it most.

Prayer: *God, grant me wisdom to understand and respond to the changes I see in my loved one. When transitions feel overwhelming, help me find strength in Your unchanging presence. May I have the discernment to identify new needs and adapt my care with compassion. In times of uncertainty, remind me that You remain constant even as abilities change. Help me treasure precious moments while preparing for the road ahead. May my heart stay steady as I witness cognitive changes in my loved one. When circumstances evolve, grant me grace to adjust my caregiving with understanding. Let Your wisdom guide me in providing the right support at the right time. In gratitude for Your faithful presence through every stage, I trust Your leading. Amen.*

Knowledge of the stages of cognitive decline empowers you to provide more effective and compassionate care for your loved one. Knowing what to expect can help you prepare for transitions while treasuring present moments. While each person's journey is unique, recognizing common patterns helps you adapt your caregiving approach with greater confidence. By understanding each stage, you can anticipate needs and respond with practical support and tender care, creating an environment that honors the challenges and the opportunities of each phase.

While Alzheimer's disease is the most common form, there are several other types, each with its own characteristics and patterns of progression. This chapter will explore the general stages most typical of Alzheimer's disease, recognizing that each person's experience may not fit neatly into these categories.

1. **Early Stage: Mild Cognitive Changes**
   Common experiences during this stage:
   - Memory lapses, especially with recent information
   - Difficulty with complex tasks
   - Subtle mood changes
   - Word-finding challenges

   Behaviors that may emerge:
   - Repetitive questions
   - Anxiety about memory lapses
   - Withdrawal from social situations
   - Resistance to help

2. **Middle Stage: Increasing Care Needs**
   Common experiences during this stage:
   - Significant memory gaps
   - Confusion about time and place
   - Changes in sleep patterns
   - Difficulty with daily tasks

   Behaviors that may emerge:
   - Wandering
   - Sundowning (increased confusion in late afternoon/evening)
   - Suspicion or paranoia
   - Agitation with personal care

3. **Late Stage: Extensive Care Needs**
   Common experiences during this stage:
   - Limited verbal communication
   - Difficulty with physical movement
   - Changes in sleep patterns
   - Complete dependence for care

Behaviors that may emerge:

- Resistance to care
- Difficulty swallowing
- Changes in awareness
- Non-verbal expressions of needs

Some key points about variability in progression:

1. Some individuals may experience rapid changes, while others may have slower progression over many years.

2. It's possible for a person to seem to "skip" a stage, moving from mild symptoms to more severe ones more quickly than expected.

3. Day-to-day fluctuations in cognitive ability and symptoms are common. A person might have "good days" and "bad days," which can sometimes mask the overall progression.

4. Some individuals may experience periods where symptoms seem to stabilize temporarily before progressing further.

5. Not everyone will experience all the symptoms associated with each stage. The order in which symptoms appear can also vary.

Recognizing this variability can help adapt expectations and care strategies.

Use this information to have important conversations about your loved one's wishes for care and to make the most of their current abilities.

There are apps available that can help track symptoms and progression. These can be useful tools for monitoring changes over time and share information with healthcare providers.

1. **Cognitive Support:**
   - Brain training apps: Games and puzzles designed to provide mental stimulation
   - Reminder apps: Help with daily tasks, medication schedules, and appointments
   - Digital calendars: Can help track days and upcoming events

2. **Safety and Security:**
   - GPS trackers: Wearable devices to help locate a person who may wander
   - Smart home systems: Can automate lighting, temperature control, and even lock doors
   - Medical alert systems: Allow quick access to help in case of falls or emergency

3. **Communication Aids:**
   - Picture phones: Make it easier to stay in touch with family and friends
   - Speech-to-text apps: Can help with writing emails or messages
   - Video calling: Allows face-to-face communication even from a distance

4. **Daily Living Assistance:**
   - Automatic pill dispensers: Help manage medication schedules
   - Smart appliances: Can shut off automatically to prevent accidents
   - Voice-activated assistants: Can help with simple tasks and provide information

5. **Engagement and Entertainment:**
    - Music streaming services: Can create personalized playlists of favorite songs
    - Virtual reality experiences: Offer immersive, safe ways to "visit" new places
    - Digital photo frames: Display a rotating collection of family photos

6. **Care Partner Support:**
    - Care coordination apps: Help multiple caregivers stay informed and organized
    - Online support groups: Provide connection with others in similar situations
    - Telehealth platforms: Allow for remote consultations with healthcare providers

When introducing new technology, it's important to do so gradually and with patience.

Choose devices that are intuitive and user-friendly. Be prepared to offer plenty of support and encouragement. As symptoms progress, simpler devices or non-tech solutions may become more appropriate.

Seek professional support. Regular check-ins with healthcare providers are crucial as cognitive impairment progresses. They can provide stage-specific advice, help manage symptoms, and connect you and your loved one with resources and support services.

Tips for navigating the stages:

1. Prioritize routine and structure in daily life. Consistency can provide a sense of security and reduce anxiety.

2. Focus on maintaining independence wherever possible. Encourage participation in daily tasks, even if they take longer to complete.

3. Create a safe environment by removing hazards and adding safety features like grab bars or motion-sensor lights.

4. Use clear, simple communication. Speak slowly, maintain eye contact, and use visual cues when necessary.

5. Engage in activities that promote cognitive stimulation and bring joy. This could be listening to music, looking at family photos, or engaging in simple crafts.

6. Prioritize physical health through regular exercise, a balanced diet, and proper sleep hygiene.

7. Stay socially connected. Encourage visits from family and friends and consider joining support groups.

8. Be patient and flexible. Some days will be better than others, so it's important to adapt your approach as needed.

9. Take care of yourself as you care for your loved one. Regular respite breaks are crucial for maintaining your own health and well-being.

These tips are not one-size-fits-all solutions; they should be adapted to your situation and the specific needs of the person dealing with cognitive changes.

Each stage brings its own challenges, but also opportunities for connection, growth, and expressions of love. By approaching each day with patience, compassion, and these practical strategies, you can help ensure the best possible quality of life for both of you. Understanding these stages helps you anticipate and prepare for changes.

DAILY CARE STRATEGIES

Chapter 4: Managing Daily Activities

Scripture: "Let all things be done decently and in order." (1 Corinthians 14:40, KJV)

As your loved one navigates changes in their daily routines, your guidance and support can help them find renewed purpose and connection with familiar tasks. Start with a basic daily structure, but stay flexible. You can follow your routine closely some days and adjust it on others. The goal is to find what helps you be most effective.

Devotional: God's wisdom teaches us that order brings peace, yet His grace shows us how to remain flexible within that structure. Through His guidance, we learn to transform daily routines into sacred moments of connection and care. When tasks feel overwhelming, He helps us break them into manageable steps, providing the patience we need to support our loved ones with tenderness. As we seek His wisdom, we discover that even the simplest activities can become channels of His love. In creating daily rhythms that honor structure and flexibility, we reflect God's perfect balance of order and grace. Trust that He guides your hands and heart, helping you discern when to maintain routine and when to adapt with understanding.

Prayer: *God, guide me as I create structure in our days while remaining flexible to changing needs. When faced with challenging tasks, help me cultivate* *patience and creative solutions. Grant me the wisdom to know when to offer help and when to foster independence. Remind me that You provide fresh strength for each new day. Help me see purpose in every activity we share, no matter how simple. Let these daily tasks become channels of Your love and care. In gratitude for Your guidance through each moment, I trust Your leading. Amen.*

Within the framework of daily routines lies opportunity for practical care and meaningful connection. As you adapt tasks and create supportive structures, remember that God's strength and wisdom are present in every moment.

Challenge: Creating a daily routine that balances structure and flexibility while accommodating changing abilities and preferences.

Solution: Develop a flexible daily schedule that includes a mix of familiar and new activities, with built-in breaks and opportunities for choice. Adapt activities as needed in the moment, focusing on the experience rather than the result.

Example: Plan a morning that includes a favorite breakfast, a short walk, and a simple household chore. If your loved one becomes tired or disengaged, suggest a break or an alternative activity they enjoy.

Tips for managing daily activities:

1. Establish a flexible routine that provides structure while allowing for spontaneity. This balance can help reduce anxiety and create a sense of normalcy.

2. Break tasks into smaller, manageable steps. This approach can prevent overwhelming your loved one and foster a sense of accomplishment.

3. Focus on abilities rather than limitations. Encourage participation in activities that align with your loved one's current skills and interests, adapting as needed.
4. Create a supportive environment by minimizing distractions and ensuring necessary items are easily accessible. This can help reduce frustration and promote independence.

5. Use clear, simple communication when providing instructions or asking questions. Visual cues and gentle reminders can be helpful.

6. Incorporate meaningful activities that connect to your loved one's life story and passions. This might include looking at photo albums, listening to favorite music, or engaging in simplified versions of favorite hobbies.

7. Prioritize physical activity and sensory experiences. Even simple exercises or nature walks can improve mood and sleep quality.

8. Be flexible and willing to adapt. Some days will be better than others, so adjust your expectations and approach accordingly.

9. Find joy in the process rather than focusing solely on outcomes. A shared laugh or a moment of connection is just as valuable as a completed task.

10. Take care of yourself. Regular breaks, self-care, and seeking support from others are crucial for maintaining your own well-being and ability to provide care.

It's the small, seemingly insignificant moments that often hold the greatest meaning. A shared smile over a morning cup of coffee, a gentle touch while folding laundry together, or a remembered lyric to a favorite song.

As you faithfully support your loved one through daily routines, remember staying patient makes a profound difference. Each day brings its own rhythm of care, challenges, and opportunities for connection. Trust that God's grace is sufficient for each task, change, and moment of patience required.

Chapter 5: Nutrition and Meal Planning

Scripture: "Whether therefore ye eat, or drink, or whatsoever ye do, do all to the glory of God." (1 Corinthians 10:31, KJV)

As you take care of your loved one each day, know that making and sharing meals is a meaningful way to show your care and support. Every meal you provide is an act of love that makes a real difference in their life.

Devotional: God provides wisdom to adapt as your loved one's needs and abilities change. Through His grace, you learn to transform simple meals into moments of connection and comfort. He gives you creativity to adjust textures, flavors, and presentation, ensuring that each dish meets physical and emotional needs. When mealtimes become challenging, trust that God is present, helping you find innovative solutions to make food appealing and manageable. As you seek His guidance in the kitchen, let His peace steady your heart.

Prayer: *God, grant me wisdom as I plan and prepare nourishing meals for my loved one. When changing abilities require alternative approaches, equip me with patience, understanding, and creativity. Help me craft dishes that are nutritious and delightful, reflecting Your loving care in every bite. In times of mealtime challenges, remind me that You are the ultimate source of strength and provision. May the meals we share become opportunities for connection, comfort, and the experience of Your gracious* *presence. I trust in Your daily guidance and give thanks for the privilege of nourishing my loved one. Amen.*

Proper nutrition is essential for supporting your loved one's physical health, cognitive function, energy levels, and emotional well-being. While the responsibility of meal planning and preparation may feel daunting, know your efforts make a significant difference in your loved one's overall well-being.

Mealtimes provide wonderful opportunities for connection and routine. Try to create a calm and friendly atmosphere that promotes socialization and relaxation. Simplifying table settings can help reduce confusion and make the dining experience more enjoyable for everyone. If your loved one struggles with regular utensils, consider introducing adaptive ones to support their independence.

Eating together can be a joyful experience, even if meals don't always go as planned. It's a chance to share time, create positive routines, and enjoy each other's company. As you prepare and share meals, fully engage your senses. Notice the colors of the food, breathe in the aromas, savor the flavors, and appreciate the different textures. These mindful moments can transform mealtimes into opportunities for gratitude and presence.

When caring for a loved one, meal planning and preparation can sometimes feel overwhelming, especially when juggling many responsibilities. Remember that you don't need to aim for perfection with every meal. The most important things are providing nourishment and creating enjoyable moments together. It's okay to simplify where you can, using healthy pre-prepared foods or accepting help from friends and family. Preparing meals may be a new role for you. It's okay to ask for help in this area by either having friends or family show you how or ask them to prepare meals for you. These are smart strategies that can give you more quality time with your loved one.

Be kind to yourself. It's natural to feel frustrated or overwhelmed when trying to meet your loved one's changing nutritional needs.

Challenge: Finding the energy and time to prepare nutritious meals while juggling caregiving responsibilities.

Solution: Streamline meal planning and preparation by focusing on simple, nutrient-dense recipes that can be made in larger batches. Accept offers of help from friends and family, and consider using a meal delivery service on especially busy days.

Example: Feeling overwhelmed by the constant need to prepare meals, you reach out to your community for support. Ask friends or family to take turns delivering homemade dinners three times a week, easing your workload and providing nourishing options for you and your loved one.

Tips for Nourishing Meals and Mealtime Connections:

1. Plan nutrient-dense meals that cater to your loved one's dietary needs, preferences, and abilities. Focus on foods that are healthy and enjoyable.

2. Make mealtimes visually appealing by using colorful ingredients, attractive plating, and thoughtful table settings. A pleasing presentation can stimulate appetite and interest.

3. Adapt food textures as needed to ensure safe and comfortable eating. Experiment with pureeing, chopping, or mashing to create manageable yet flavorful dishes.

4. Use herbs, spices, and seasonings to enhance taste without relying heavily on salt or sugar. Be open to trying new flavor combinations that tantalize the senses.

5. Create a calm, inviting atmosphere by minimizing distractions, playing soft music, and engaging in pleasant conversation during meals.

6. Involve your loved one in meal preparation, when possible, even if it's just small tasks. This can provide a sense of purpose, stimulate appetite, and create meaningful moments together.

7. Prioritize your own nutrition as well. Accept help from others, simplify meal routines when needed, and make time for nourishing yourself physically and emotionally.

8. Encourage hydration by offering fluids throughout the day in various forms, such as water, juice, soups, or foods with high water content. Keep water easily accessible and use clear containers to monitor intake.

Above all, let each meal be infused with love and care. As you navigate the challenges and joys of nourishing your loved one, trust in God's presence and provision. Embrace the opportunity to transform daily sustenance into a sacred experience—one bite, one sip, and one shared moment at a time.

During the challenges and responsibilities of caregiving, let mealtimes serve as reminders of God's constant love and provision.

Chapter 6: Encouraging Physical Activity

Scripture: "I will praise thee; for I am fearfully and wonderfully made." (Psalm 139:14, KJV)

Take each day as it comes when helping your loved one stay active. You'll find ways to adjust movements that work for them, and every bit of activity makes a difference. It's important to keep them moving in ways that feel comfortable and safe. Together, you can discover new ways to transform simple movements into moments of connection and joy, strengthening your bond with each shared experience.

Devotional: God creates our bodies with a remarkable capacity for movement and vitality. Through His grace, you learn to encourage physical activity that nurtures the body and spirit. As abilities shift, God guides you in finding fresh approaches to maintain mobility and strength. He gives you creativity to discover exercises that bring shared joy and celebrate the gift of life. Trust that in every gentle walk, stretch, or activity you share, God's design for physical wellness flows through your supportive care.

Prayer: *God, grant me wisdom to encourage physical activity that brings health and joy to both my loved one and myself. When abilities change, help me adapt with understanding and creativity. Give me strength to maintain my physical wellness while supporting others. In times of fatigue, remind me that You renew our energy each day. Help me see movement as a celebration of Your gift of life. When* *exercise becomes challenging, grant me patience to find new ways to stay active. In gratitude for the gift of movement, I trust Your guidance. Amen.*

Movement brings joy and connection to both of your lives. Help your loved one stay active in whatever ways work best—whether it's gentle stretches, short walks, or simple exercises together. Taking care of their physical health and your own makes a real difference. Remember that even small activities matter and can brighten your day together.

Regular movement helps—it can boost mood, improve sleep, and support health. Find activities that your loved one enjoys, and be creative - exercise can be pulling weeds, hanging laundry to dry, or washing windows, not just short walks or gentle stretches. When you exercise together, you both benefit—it helps reduce stress and creates special moments between you. Start with what feels comfortable and know that every bit of movement counts.

Regular movement keeps muscles strong, improves balance, and makes daily tasks easier. It can boost mood, help you sleep better, and give you more energy throughout the day.

When you're active, even in small ways, you feel a sense of accomplishment. Moving more helps you feel connected and positive.

Challenge: Balancing the demands of caregiving with finding time for personal physical activity.

Solution: Look for opportunities to integrate physical activity into daily routines and make it a shared experience when possible. Prioritize self-care through movement, recognizing its importance for personal well-being and the ability to provide effective care.

Example: You know you should exercise more, but it feels like there's never enough time with all the caregiving responsibilities. Besides working out together, try scheduling a regular walking date each week with a friend. You can catch up while getting some movement in, and it can be a dedicated time for you to focus on your own health.

Tips for Incorporating Physical Activity:

1. Choose activities that align with your loved one's current abilities and interests, adapting as needed.

2. Start small and celebrate each achievement, focusing on the joy and sense of accomplishment.

3. Make physical activity a regular part of daily life, integrating it into existing routines when possible.

4. Ensure a safe environment for exercise, providing necessary support and supervision.

5. Encourage social engagement through group activities or exercising with friends and family.

6. Focus on the present moment during physical activity, promoting mindfulness and stress reduction.

7. Lead by example, prioritizing your own physical health and well-being as a care partner.

8. Be patient, flexible, and attuned to your loved one's changing needs and preferences.

Physical activity is about far more than just promoting physical fitness. It's about nurturing the mind, body, and spirit through movement. It's about fostering independence, self-esteem, and social connection. Most importantly, it's about embracing the joy and vitality that can be found in the present moment, regardless of the challenges faced.

Chapter 7: Addressing Sleep Issues

Scripture: "I will both lay me down in peace, and sleep: for thou, Lord, only makest me dwell in safety." (Psalm 4:8, KJV)

Nighttime care can be challenging, but you can create peaceful bedtime routines that help everyone rest better. Focus on simple, calming activities before bed. Remember that taking breaks and getting rest yourself is just as important.

Devotional: In the quiet hours when sleep proves elusive, God provides His steadfast presence and strength. Through His grace, you learn to navigate changing sleep patterns with patience and wisdom. He gives you discernment to create calming environments that soothes body and spirit. When nighttime care leaves you exhausted, trust that God sustains you, offering moments of rest even in broken sleep.

As you seek His guidance in managing sleep challenges, let His peace calm anxious nights. Remember that in every midnight vigil, God's faithful care encompasses you and your loved one, bringing comfort in the darkness.

Prayer: God, grant us peaceful rest tonight. *When sleep becomes fragmented, help me find renewal in Your presence. Give me wisdom to create calming routines that bring rest to my loved one and myself. In times of exhaustion, remind me that You provide strength for each new day. Help me establish rhythms that promote restful sleep. When nights feel endless,* *grant me patience and endurance. Let these hours of darkness become wrapped in Your peace. In gratitude for Your constant watch over us, I trust Your care. Amen.*

Addressing sleep issues can be a complex and emotionally taxing process. The demands of providing round-the-clock care, coupled with the stress and exhaustion of disrupted sleep, can leave you feeling overwhelmed and drained. It's essential to approach this challenge with patience, compassion, and a willingness to seek support from healthcare professionals and other caregivers who have navigated similar experiences.

One key strategy is to create a comfortable sleep environment that promotes relaxation. This may include keeping the bedroom cool, dark, and quiet, using supportive pillows and bedding, and considering tools like blackout curtains to minimize disruptions. Establishing a consistent bedtime routine that incorporates calming activities, such as reading, listening to soothing music, or engaging in gentle stretches, can also help signal to the body and mind that it's time to prepare for rest.

It's crucial to identify and manage factors that may contribute to sleep disturbances. This might involve working with healthcare providers to adjust medication dosages or timing to minimize sleep-disrupting side effects, ensuring adequate exposure to natural light during the day to regulate the body's internal clock, and encouraging regular physical activity to improve sleep quality and duration. Be sure to choose activities that are appropriate for your loved one's abilities and preferences.

For those adjusting to cognitive changes, sleep disturbances can be particularly frustrating and disorienting. The blurring of day and night, paired with feelings of confusion and anxiety, can make it difficult to find rest and peace. Validating these experiences and offering reassurance that you're there to provide comfort and support through the challenges is essential. Simple gestures like holding hands, offering soothing words, or gently rubbing their back can convey love and security during difficult moments.

It's equally important to validate your own emotional experiences and the toll that a lack of sleep can have on your well-being. You may feel guilty or inadequate when unable to soothe your loved one's restlessness, or experience frustration and exhaustion from ongoing disruptions. These feelings are normal and understandable. Remember to prioritize self-care by enlisting the help of family, friends, or respite services to provide breaks for rest and renewal.

> **Challenge:** Feeling overwhelmed and exhausted due to frequently interrupted sleep.
>
> **Solution:** Prioritize self-care by enlisting the help of family, friends, or respite services to provide breaks for rest and renewal. Establish a consistent daily routine with clear cues for waking and sleeping times, using light therapy or exposure to natural sunlight to help regulate the body's internal clock.

Example: Your loved one may have difficulty distinguishing between day and night, leading to confusion and agitation.

- Try maintaining a consistent daily routine. Every morning at the same time, open the curtains wide and have breakfast by the window to get some natural sunlight.
- Stay active throughout the day with regular activities.
- As evening approaches, start dimming the lights and switch to calmer activities.
- An hour before bed, begin your bedtime routine, closing curtains, putting on comfortable pajamas, and perhaps listening to soft music.
- If there is trouble settling down, try using a small light therapy lamp for about 30 minutes in the morning to help set the body's clock.

Tips for Managing Sleep Issues:

1. Establish a consistent bedtime routine that includes calming activities like reading, listening to soothing music, or gentle stretches.

2. Create a comfortable sleep environment by keeping the bedroom cool, dark, and quiet. Consider using supportive pillows, blackout

curtains, or white noise machines to minimize disruptions.

3. Manage factors that may contribute to sleep disturbances, such as medication timing or caffeine intake. Work with healthcare providers to adjust medication dosages or schedules to minimize sleep-disrupting side effects.

4. Encourage regular physical activity during the day, choosing activities appropriate for your loved one's abilities and preferences.

5. Ensure adequate exposure to natural light during the day to help regulate the body's internal clock. Light therapy may be beneficial if outdoor exposure is limited.

6. Limit daytime napping to no more than 30 minutes and avoid napping late in the afternoon, as this can interfere with nighttime sleep.

7. Practice relaxation techniques together, such as deep breathing exercises or gentle massage, to promote calmness before bedtime.

8. Address any underlying health issues that may contribute to sleep disturbances, such as pain, heartburn, or sleep apnea. Regular check-ups with healthcare providers can help identify and manage these concerns.

9. Consider using assistive devices or technology, such as bed alarms or motion sensors, to ensure safety during nighttime wandering while allowing for more restful sleep for care partners.

Addressing sleep issues is a process that may require time and adjustments. Be patient with yourselves, celebrating small improvements and seeking support when needed. With consistent effort, compassion, and faith, you can work towards more restful nights and better overall well-being for you and your loved one.

COMMUNICATION AND CONNECTION

Chapter 8: Navigating Communication Challenges

Scripture: "A word fitly spoken is like apples of gold in pitchers of silver." (Proverbs 25:11, KJV)

Supporting someone when communication changes takes patience, but there are many ways to stay connected. Watch for facial expressions, gentle touches, and other signs that show how they're feeling. Your calm presence and caring attention mean so much, even when words are hard to find.

Devotional: Through God's love, you learn to recognize the sacred language of touch, expression, and shared moments of quiet. When words become difficult, His spirit helps you bridge the gap with understanding and grace. God sees your efforts to adapt and communicate in new ways, blessing each attempt to maintain connection. Trust that His presence flows through every gesture of care, every patient response, and every moment of understanding you share with your loved one. Remember that communication is more than words—it's about the love that binds hearts together.

Prayer: *God, guide me in finding new ways to connect and communicate with my loved one. Grant me patience when words become challenging, wisdom to understand unspoken needs, and creativity in finding new paths to share meaning. Help me listen not just with my ears, but with my heart. When frustration rises, calm my spirit and remind me that* *love speaks in many languages. Give me strength to remain present in difficult moments and joy in finding new ways to connect. Let my presence bring comfort even in silence, and help me find peace in our shared understanding. Amen.*

As you witness changes in your loved one's communication abilities, your patience and understanding become powerful tools in maintaining your connection. Effective communication isn't just about words—it's about presence, patience, and the willingness to connect in whatever way works best for each of you.

While verbal skills may decline, the need for meaningful interaction remains as vital as ever. You can convey and interpret messages by using nonverbal cues, body language, and tone of voice. Active listening, clear and slow speech, and simple, direct language create an environment of understanding and respect. A gentle touch, a reassuring presence, and a patient ear communicate love.

If you notice your loved one struggling to express themselves verbally, try paying closer attention to their facial expressions and gestures. A smile or a frustrated frown is a form of communication. Spend time focusing on non-verbal cues and practice expressing yourself non-verbally as well.

Instead of asking open-ended questions, offer clear choices. For example, instead of "What would you like to eat?" you can ask "Would you like an apple or an orange?" Break down complex sentences into simpler, shorter phrases. Resist the urge to correct or argue; instead, validate your loved one's feelings and redirect conversations to more positive topics.

When your loved one repeatedly asks about a deceased friend or relative, you can **validate** the emotion ("I can see you're missing Mom"), **redirect** to a related topic ("She loved gardening."), and then **distract** with an activity ("Shall we look at her garden photos?").

As verbal abilities change, explore alternative forms of expression. Art, music, and movement offer powerful outlets for emotions and memories that may be difficult to articulate. Embrace these creative channels as a means of self-expression and connection.

Patience is a virtue for all involved in the face of communication challenges. Allow ample time for responses, resisting the urge to rush or interrupt. Celebrate the small victories, like a shared smile or a moment of recognition, and let go of perfectionistic expectations.

Acknowledge any feelings of frustration, sadness, or helplessness with compassion. Give your loved one ample time to process your words and formulate their responses. Speak slowly, clearly, and in short, simple sentences. Use a gentle, reassuring tone and minimize distractions in the environment.

Maintain eye contact and use friendly facial expressions and gestures to show your interest and engagement. If your loved one becomes frustrated or agitated, respond with compassion and validation. Offer reassurance and support.

> **Challenge:** Feeling frustrated or helpless when communication becomes difficult, despite your best efforts.

Solution: Acknowledge your feelings with compassion and remind yourself that your presence and efforts make a difference. Seek support from others who understand the challenges you face, and prioritize self-care to maintain your emotional well-being.

Example: You notice your loved one becomes agitated during conversations in the busy living room. Try shifting important talks to a quiet bedroom. This may allow for calmer, more productive interactions. Identify the most calming space in your home and have your next important conversation there, noting any differences in communication quality.

Tips for Communicating:

1. Embrace non-verbal communication. Pay attention to and use body language and tone of voice.

2. Adapt your communication style. Speak slowly, clearly, and use simple, direct language.

3. Create a supportive communication environment. Minimize distractions and foster a calm atmosphere for conversations.

4. Implement the **"Validate, Redirect, Distract"** technique when addressing repetitive questions or concerns.

5. Explore alternative forms of expression. Incorporate art, music, touch, and shared activities as forms of connection.

6. Consider using communication apps designed for individuals dealing with brain health issues which often include picture-based communication boards or simplified interfaces.

7. Seek professional support. Speech and language therapists can provide valuable strategies tailored to your specific communication challenges.

By embracing non-verbal cues, adapting communication styles, and exploring alternative forms of expression, you can continue to foster meaningful connections. Remember, your love and dedication are the foundation of your communication, and every effort you make to connect is a precious gift.

Chapter 9: Engaging in Meaningful Activities

Scripture: "And whatsoever ye do, do it heartily, as to the Lord, and not unto men." (Colossians 3:23, KJV)

Spending time with your loved one is a gift—even the smallest moments can bring you closer together. Whether you're sharing a meal, looking at photos, or simply holding hands, these daily activities create special memories for both of you. Remember that you don't have to do anything complicated. The simple act of being present and showing your love makes each moment meaningful.

Devotional: God sees your efforts to create meaningful moments, whether through familiar routines or new experiences together. When activities don't unfold as planned, His presence reminds you that the heart behind each effort matters most. God rejoices in your dedication to nurturing your loved one's sense of purpose and well-being.

Prayer: *God, help me see the beauty in simple moments shared with my loved one. Grant me creativity to adapt activities as abilities change, and wisdom to recognize joy in new ways of engaging. Give me patience when tasks take longer and understanding when interests shift. Help me find meaning in our shared activities, whether familiar or new. When I feel overwhelmed by planning and adapting, renew my energy and inspire fresh ideas. Thank You for each moment of connection, each shared smile, and each small victory we celebrate together. Guide us in finding purpose and delight in our daily activities. Amen.*

For individuals confronting cognitive challenges, engaging in familiar tasks or exploring new interests provides a sense of accomplishment and helps maintain identity. For care partners, facilitating these activities offers opportunities for positive interaction and shared experiences that strengthen the bond between them.

When planning activities, focus on the process rather than the outcome, adapting tasks to your loved one's current abilities and interests. What makes an activity meaningful can change over time, so remain flexible and attentive to what brings them satisfaction and engagement in the present moment.

One key aspect of meaningful engagement is tapping into activities that resonate with your loved one's lifelong hobbies, interests, or professional skills. These familiar pursuits can evoke deep-rooted memories and provide a comforting sense of continuity. For example, a person who has always enjoyed gardening may find great joy in tending to a small indoor plant or herb garden. A former musician might light up when given the chance to play a simplified version of a favorite song on the piano or listen to favorite recordings.

As memory changes progress, adapt activities to match your loved one's abilities. This doesn't mean abandoning cherished hobbies altogether, but rather finding ways to modify them into more manageable forms. A complex knitting pattern can be simplified to basic stitches, or a multi-step recipe can be broken down into a few key ingredients.

What matters most is enjoying your time together, not getting things perfect. The simple joy of doing something side by side is what makes these moments special.

Try new things together—maybe painting with bright colors, shaping clay with your hands, or arranging beautiful flowers. You might enjoy gentle movement, like swaying to favorite songs or doing easy stretches in a chair. Take it slow and see what brings a smile.

Sometimes, it's difficult when activities that once came easily become more challenging. It's completely natural to experience sadness about these changes. Focus on simply being together in the moment—notice the bright colors around you, explore the variety of textures, listen to soothing sounds, and share your thoughts. The true gift lies in these shared moments—the laughter, the warm glances, and the closeness of being with someone you love.

Challenge: Finding the time and energy to plan and facilitate meaningful activities while juggling other caregiving responsibilities.

Solution: Start small, looking for opportunities to weave activities into your existing daily routines. Reach out to friends, family members, or community resources for support and fresh ideas.

Example: Knowing your loved one enjoys music but struggling to find dedicated listening time, try making it part of your everyday routine. Play favorite songs while doing household chores together or create a special playlist for your morning coffee time. Those little moments of shared joy can make a big impact.

Tips for Engaging in Meaningful Activities:

1. Focus on activities that align with your loved one's current abilities and interests.

2. Break tasks into smaller, manageable steps to avoid frustration.

3. Emphasize the process and the enjoyment over the end result.

4. Look for opportunities to weave activities into your daily routine.

5. Tap into lifelong hobbies, interests, or professional skills for a sense of continuity.

6. Be open to trying new things and adapting as needed.

7. Celebrate the small victories and moments of connection.

8. Remember, your presence and efforts are profoundly meaningful.

Every moment you spend together is precious, whether you're trying something new or just enjoying quiet company. Don't worry about doing things perfectly. What matters is being together and finding little bits of joy along the way. Start with small, easy activities and give yourself time to find what works best. Even the simplest things, like humming an old tune or sharing a gentle touch, can fill your day with meaning.

Some of life's most beautiful moments are the quiet ones—like taking a slow walk together on a nice day, singing songs that bring back happy memories, or just sitting close and holding hands. These simple moments show how deep your love runs and how special your connection is, no matter what life brings your way.

Chapter 10: Creating Meaningful Moments

Scripture: "A merry heart doeth good like a medicine: but a broken spirit drieth the bones." (Proverbs 17:22, KJV)

Even the smallest moments you share are special gifts—whether you're enjoying a meal together or taking a quiet walk side by side. These simple daily activities become precious times of joyful connection. Trust that you'll find your way to what feels right and meaningful for you and your loved one each day.

Devotional: Through God's wisdom, you learn to see beyond tasks to the sacred moments of bonding they contain. Trust that He guides you in discovering new ways to bring delight to your loved one's day. When activities don't go as planned, His grace reminds you that perfect outcomes matter less than loving presence. God sees your efforts to create moments of joy, and He multiplies their impact in ways you may not see. Remember that each smile, each shared activity, each moment of connection is precious in His sight. Let His joy flow through you as you discover creative ways to strengthen your bond and create lasting memories together.

Prayer: *God, guide me in creating moments of meaning and joy with my loved one. Grant me the wisdom to see opportunities for connection in everyday moments, and the patience to embrace the process rather than focus on outcomes. When I feel overwhelmed by the challenges, remind me that even the smallest shared experience can bring unexpected* *delight. Help me remain present in each moment, finding peace in simple activities and joy in our time together. Give me creativity to discover new ways to engage, flexibility to adapt when needed, and grace to accept that perfect moments don't require perfect circumstances. Let my presence bring comfort and joy, and help me find renewal in our shared experiences. In gratitude for these precious moments, I rest in Your peace. Amen.*

The most beautiful moments often come from simply being together—whether you're looking through old photos, sharing a song, or just holding hands. It's not about doing things perfectly. It's about those small, precious times when you connect with each other.

Think about what brings a smile to your loved one's face. Perhaps it's listening to their favorite songs from years ago or flipping through family photo albums together. These activities do more than just fill time; they help your loved one feel valued and understood. Each shared memory and story helps keep their spirit bright.

You can find joy in creative moments, too. Whether it's painting, singing, or telling stories, these activities let you both express yourselves freely. And don't overlook the value of everyday tasks—folding warm laundry together, setting the table, or watching flowers grow in a small garden can bring unexpected moments of connection.

Remember that some days will be easier than others, and that's okay. What matters is being there together, adjusting as needed, and finding ways to share little moments of joy. Watch for what makes your loved one's eyes light up—sometimes the simplest things bring the most happiness.

Challenge: Finding the time and energy to initiate engaging activities while managing the demands of daily care.

Solution: Start small and incorporate activities into your existing routine. Look for opportunities to turn everyday moments into chances for connection and engagement.

Example: While preparing a meal together, engage your loved one in simple tasks like washing vegetables or setting the table. Use this time to reminisce about favorite family recipes or memorable meals.

Tips for creating meaningful moments:

1. Focus on the process, not the outcome: Enjoy the activity itself rather than worrying about the end result.

2. Tap into existing interests and abilities: Choose activities that align with your loved one's past hobbies and skills.

3. Share precious memories together by looking at old photos, playing songs that bring back happy times, or just talking about favorite stories from

the past. These special moments help you stay close and often bring unexpected smiles and joy.

4. Explore creative pursuits: Engage in art, music, or storytelling as forms of expression and communication.

5. Incorporate everyday tasks: Find meaning in simple activities like folding laundry or setting the table.

6. Remain flexible and adaptable: Be willing to modify activities as needed, based on your loved one's responses.

7. Create a supportive environment: Offer praise and encouragement, focusing on efforts rather than limitations.

8. Consider social activities: Participate in dementia-friendly group activities to foster a sense of community.

9. Start small and integrate into routines: Look for opportunities to turn everyday moments into chances for connection.

10. Embrace imperfection: It's the shared experience and attempt to connect that matters most.

Every day brings fresh chances to share special moments together. Just being there with an open heart, whether you're sharing a meal or a gentle smile, creates memories to treasure. Trust that each small moment you share—even the quiet ones—brings you closer together and fills your hearts with joy. Let your love and faith guide you as you find new ways to make each day meaningful.

EMOTIONAL WELL-BEING

Chapter 11: The Power of Self-Compassion

Scripture: "For I will satisfy the weary soul, and every languishing soul I will replenish." (Jeremiah 31:25, KJV)

When you're feeling tired from caring for others, remember to be gentle with yourself too. Taking care of yourself is a precious gift that helps you stay strong. Trust that you're supported and loved as you give so much of yourself to others.

Devotional: God's love for you remains constant, unaffected by your performance or productivity. He delights when you take time to rest and replenish your spirit, knowing this nurtures the care you provide to others. Trust that He understands your challenges and provides strength when you feel depleted. In moments of self-doubt, remember that His compassion flows through you, teaching you to be gentle with yourself. God's care for you is unlimited—let His example guide you in showing the same tenderness to yourself that you offer others. Your worth in His eyes never wavers, and His presence brings refreshment to your weary soul.

Prayer: *God, help me remember that caring for myself is as vital as caring for others. When weariness settles in my bones, guide me to moments of rest and renewal. Grant me the wisdom to treat* *myself with the same compassion I offer to others, and the courage to acknowledge my own needs. In times of self-doubt, help me find strength in gentleness and power in self-acceptance. May I learn to embrace imperfection with grace, finding peace in knowing that my best efforts are enough. Guide me to recognize the small moments where I can pause, breathe, and nurture my own spirit. Let me find balance between giving and receiving, action and rest, care for others and care for self. In the quiet moments of each day, help me remember that my own well-being is a precious gift worth tending. With gratitude for this journey of growth and understanding, I rest in Your peace. Amen.*

Your ability to care for others flows from the well of kindness you offer yourself. In practicing self-compassion, you create the resilience and strength needed to face each day with renewed purpose and grace.

Tasks can sometimes feel overwhelming, leading to exhaustion, self-doubt, or guilt. Think of self-compassion as the oxygen mask you must put on first before helping others. Try incorporating brief moments of self-care into your daily routine. While helping your loved one, take a moment to mentally "wash away" any negative thoughts about yourself, replacing them with kind and supportive ones. Begin your day with a few deep breaths, affirming your own worth and strength.

Self-compassion is a powerful tool for navigating the challenges you face. It involves treating yourself with the same kindness and understanding you'd offer a good friend. Throughout each day, try to pause briefly to reconnect with your inner sense of compassion. These moments of self-kindness, whether it's taking a short walk, listening to a favorite song, or simply acknowledging your efforts, are crucial for maintaining your well-being.

By practicing self-compassion, you build a foundation of resilience that allows you to face each day with renewed strength. It helps preserve your sense of self-worth and dignity. When frustration arises, pause and take a deep breath. Remind yourself that it's okay to find things challenging and that you're doing your best. This self-compassion can help you navigate the ups and downs with greater resilience.

Challenge: Finding time for self-compassion amidst the constant demands of caregiving.

Solution: Integrate brief moments of self-compassion into your daily caregiving routine, turning care tasks into opportunities for self-care.

Example: While preparing a meal for your loved one, take a moment to savor the aromas and appreciate your efforts. You might think, "I am nurturing my loved one and myself with this act of care."

Tips for Cultivating Self-Compassion:

1. Start each day with a self-compassion affirmation. Look in the mirror and remind yourself, "I am doing the best I can, and my efforts matter."

2. Create a self-compassion trigger. Choose an object, such as a small stone or a bracelet, to serve as a reminder to practice self-compassion throughout the day.

3. Practice self-care in small, manageable ways. Take a 5-minute break to stretch, enjoy a cup of tea, or listen to a favorite song.

4. Reframe self-critical thoughts with understanding. When you catch yourself thinking, "I should be doing more," or "I'm not good enough," pause and reframe these thoughts with compassion.

5. Practice self-compassion meditation. Take a few minutes each day to sit quietly and focus on your breath. Repeat a self-compassion mantra, such as "May I be kind to myself" or "May I accept myself as I am."

6. Seek professional support when needed. If you struggle with self-compassion or experiencing persistent feelings of self-doubt or burnout, don't hesitate to reach out to a therapist or counselor.

Self-compassion is a practice, not a destination. Be patient with yourself as you learn to incorporate these tips into your daily life. With time and consistency, self-compassion can become a powerful source of strength and resilience, helping you navigate the caregiving journey with greater grace and peace.

Chapter 12: Mindful Practice

Scripture: "Be still, and know that I am God." (Psalm 46:10, KJV)

God invites you into moments of sacred stillness. In the busyness of caregiving, He provides opportunities to pause and be fully present.

Devotional: Through God's guidance, you can find deeper awareness in each moment, whether in quiet contemplation or daily tasks. He gives you wisdom to see the holy in the ordinary—in shared meals, gentle touches, or quiet companionship. God sees your effort to remain present and patient, even when the mind wants to race ahead. Trust that He is with you in every breath, every interaction, and every moment of mindful attention. When you quiet your spirit to listen, His presence becomes clearer, helping you respond to each situation with grace and understanding. Remember that in stillness, you can know His presence more fully, finding renewal for the journey ahead.

Prayer: *God, guide me into the stillness where wisdom dwells. When my mind races with worry or tasks, help me return to the anchor of my breath and the ground of the present moment. Grant me the grace to be fully present with my loved one, to listen deeply, and to respond with patience and understanding. In times of challenge, remind me to pause and breathe, finding strength in stillness and clarity in calm. Help me embrace each moment as it comes, without judgment or resistance. May I find* *peace in simple presence, wisdom in quiet attention, and renewal in mindful awareness. When repetitive conversations arise, grant me patience to hear the heart beneath the words. Let my presence be a source of comfort and stability for my loved one, and may our shared moments be blessed with genuine connection. In gratitude for this practice of presence, I rest in Your peace. Amen.*

Mindfulness isn't about adding one more task to your day—it's about bringing quality of attention to what you're already doing. Through simple presence and gentle awareness, you can transform routine moments into opportunities for connection and peace. Remember that each return to the present moment, each mindful breath, and each conscious choice to respond rather than react strengthens your capacity for resilient, compassionate caregiving. In the practice of mindfulness, you discover that peace isn't found in perfect circumstances but in meeting each moment with an open, accepting heart.

As a care partner, mindfulness emerges as a powerful tool for you and your loved one. This practice of being fully present in the moment can transform the caregiving experience, offering benefits that extend far beyond the immediate task at hand.

Whether during a care task or a quiet moment, focus on your senses and breathing. By doing so, you can reduce anxiety and deepen your connection with your loved one. Encourage them to join you in this practice, guiding them gently through the process of noticing their surroundings and sensations.

Mindfulness in caregiving begins with a simple yet profound shift in attention. It involves bringing full awareness to the present moment, whether that's assisting with daily activities, sharing a meal, or simply sitting in quiet companionship. This focused attention allows you to notice subtle cues from your loved one, respond more effectively to their needs, and find moments of connection even as cognitive abilities decline.

Mindfulness can be a vital source of stress relief and emotional regulation. The demands of caregiving can be overwhelming, often leading to burnout and compassion fatigue. By practicing mindfulness, you can create a mental space between stimulus and response, allowing for more thoughtful, less reactive caregiving. This can lead to reduced anxiety, improved patience, and a greater sense of calm in challenging situations.

Challenge: Staying present and patient during repetitive conversations or questions.

Solution: Practice "Mindful Listening" by focusing on the emotional content behind the words, rather than the repetition itself.

Example: When your loved one asks the same question for the fifth time, take a mindful breath and respond with compassion. You might say, "I can see this is really important to you. Let's talk about it." By meeting the repetition with patience and understanding, you validate their feelings and maintain a sense of connection.

Tips for Cultivating Mindful Presence:

1. Practice “Mindful Check-ins” throughout the day. Set aside a few minutes each morning or evening to sit quietly and tune into your present experience.

2. Integrate mindfulness into daily care tasks. When assisting your loved one with activities like bathing or dressing, focus your full attention on the present moment.

3. Engage in “Mindful Communication” with your loved one. During conversations, give them your full attention. Make eye contact, listen actively, and respond with patience and understanding.

4. Practice “Mindful Listening” during repetitive conversations. When your loved one repeats questions or stories, shift your focus to the emotional content behind the words. Respond with empathy and validation.

5. Encourage mindful engagement in leisure activities. When your loved one participates in hobbies or enjoyable activities, help them fully immerse themselves in the experience.

6. Use “Mindful Pauses” to manage difficult emotions. When faced with frustration, anxiety, or stress, take a brief pause to acknowledge the emotion without judgment.

7. Cultivate self-compassion through mindfulness. When self-critical thoughts arise, practice observing them without judgment. Offer yourself the same kindness and understanding you extend to your loved one.

8. Seek out mindfulness resources and support. Explore mindfulness classes, support groups, or online resources tailored for caregivers or those with cognitive challenges.

Mindfulness is a practice, not a destination. Be patient and compassionate with yourself as you integrate these tips. Celebrate the small moments of connection and presence, and trust that every mindful step is a step towards greater peace and resilience.

Chapter 13: Finding Calm in the Storm

Scripture: "Thou wilt keep him in perfect peace, whose mind is stayed on thee: because he trusteth in thee." (Isaiah 26:3, KJV)

When caring for others feels like too much, remember that you can find peace and calm. Taking care of someone is challenging work, and it's completely normal to feel stressed and worried or even angry. In those difficult moments, pause and take comfort in knowing you're not alone—there is divine support available to help steady and center you. Your feelings are valid, and there is always hope and strength to draw upon when you need it most.

Devotional: Through God's strength, you can find moments of rest, even during busy or difficult days. He gives you wisdom to know when to step back and take a breath. God understands when caregiving demands drain your energy and helps you find ways to restore your peace. Trust that He guides you to create pockets of calm within challenging days. When you turn to Him during stressful moments, His peace helps steady your thoughts and actions. Remember that in every challenging situation, God's peace is available to strengthen and support you.

Prayer: *God, help me find peace when caregiving feels overwhelming. When I'm stressed, remind me to pause and rest in Your presence. Give me wisdom to recognize when I need to take breaks. During hard moments, help me remember that Your peace is* *always available. Guide me in caring for myself while caring for others. When anxiety rises, grant me calm to think clearly. Let Your peace flow through me to comfort my loved one. In trust that You provide the peace I need each day, I rest in Your care. Amen.*

Taking breaks is essential. Even a few quiet moments can make a real difference in how you feel and care for others. When you're less stressed, you'll notice that you and the person you care for feel more at ease.

Here's what you need to know: caregiving is demanding work that affects your whole body and mind. You might feel tired, worried, or on edge. Your sleep and appetite might change. These reactions are completely normal—you're handling a lot.

Try this: Take three deep breaths when things feel overwhelming. Step outside for fresh air. Spend five minutes doing something that makes you smile. These small actions can help you feel more centered.

> **Challenge:** You often find yourself overwhelmed by the constant demands. You struggle to find moments of peace and calm amidst the chaos, leading to increased stress and burnout.
>
> **Solution:** Implement a daily mindfulness practice to help center yourself and reduce stress. This can be as simple as a few minutes of deep breathing or meditation each day. Combined with the "3-3-3" grounding technique, this

practice can help you find moments of calm, even in challenging situations.

Example: You notice your loved one becoming agitated and repeatedly asking the same question. You feel your stress levels rising, but you remember your mindfulness practice. Take a moment to use the "3-3-3" technique:

1. Take three deep breaths, focusing on the sensation of the air moving in and out of your lungs.

2. Name three things you can see in your immediate environment.

3. Move three parts of your body, such as rolling your shoulders, wiggling your toes, and gently stretching your neck.

This brief pause helps you regain your composure. With renewed patience and compassion, you're now better equipped to respond to your loved one. You might gently redirect their attention to a calming activity you can do together, such as looking at a familiar photo album or listening to their favorite music.

Don't hesitate to reach out for help. Connect with family members, friends, or join a support group. Sharing your experiences with others who understand can provide validation and encouragement. Building a strong network of support can help you feel less alone and more equipped to handle the challenges of caregiving.

Tips for Managing Stress and Finding Peace:

1. Incorporate brief stress-reduction techniques into your daily routine, such as deep breathing exercises, progressive muscle relaxation or mindfulness meditation.

2. Create a portable “calm kit” filled with items that bring you comfort and relaxation, such as a favorite book, soothing scented lotion, calming playlist, or stress ball.

3. Practice the “3-3-3” grounding technique when feeling anxious or overwhelmed.

4. Cultivate a support network of family, friends, and fellow care partners who understand what you’re going through.

5. Prioritize self-care activities that bring you joy and relaxation, such as hobbies, exercise, spending time in nature, or connecting with others.

6. Practice self-compassion and self-forgiveness. Remind yourself that caregiving is challenging, and it’s okay to have difficult emotions or make mistakes.

7. Focus on the positive aspects of caregiving and cultivate gratitude. Reflect on the meaningful moments, lessons learned, and personal growth you’ve experienced.

8. Seek professional support when needed, such as counseling, therapy, or support groups.

Managing stress and finding calm is an ongoing practice, not a one-time achievement. Be patient and compassionate with yourself as you explore different strategies and find what works best for you. Trust in your own resilience, lean on your support network, and hold fast to the love and purpose that guides you.

Chapter 14: The Power of Building Resilience

Scripture: "But they that wait upon the Lord shall renew their strength; they shall mount up with wings as eagles; they shall run, and not be weary; and they shall walk, and not faint." (Isaiah 40:31, KJV)

When caregiving feels difficult, remember that you have deep wells of strength within you. You'll find the energy and resilience you need to face each day. Trust that there is divine support lifting you up and giving you renewed strength when you need it most.

Devotional: In times of weariness, God invites you to wait upon Him, to find rest and renewal in His presence. As you rely on His strength, He enables you to face each day with fresh courage and grace. Though the journey may feel long and tiring at times, God's power sustains you, helping you to press on without growing faint. He gives you the resilience to adapt to changes, to recover from setbacks, and to find hope in the midst of struggles. As you trust in His unfailing love and faithfulness, you discover that your strength is not limited to your own abilities, but is constantly renewed by the One who never grows weary.

Prayer: *God, I come to You today, seeking Your strength. When I feel overwhelmed by the demands and responsibilities, remind me to wait upon You, to find rest and renewal in Your presence. Help me to trust in Your promise to renew my strength. Give me the courage to face each day with resilience, knowing* *that Your grace is sufficient for every challenge. When I stumble or feel discouraged, help me to remember that my strength comes from You, and that You are always ready to lift me up again. Thank You for the gift of Your unfailing love and constant presence, which sustains me through every step of this journey. In Jesus' name I pray, Amen.*

Building strength isn't about never getting tired or overwhelmed—it's about finding practical ways to bounce back when things are tough. Every small step helps, like learning to take deep breaths when stressed, calling a friend, or simply starting fresh after a hard day. You build strength not just by pushing through challenges, but by knowing when you need to rest.

Remember that you and your loved one are on this journey together. You're both learning and adapting as you go. When things don't go as planned, it's not a failure—it's just part of the process.

Try this: Each night before bed, take a moment to write down three good things that happened that day. They can be as simple as sharing a smile or enjoying a cup of tea. This small habit helps you notice the bright spots, even on difficult days.

Challenge: Feeling overwhelmed by constant demands and responsibilities.

Solution: Break down tasks into smaller, manageable steps. Celebrate each bit of progress.

> **Example:** When the day ahead looks daunting, focus on one task at a time. Break your caregiving duties into smaller, more manageable parts. Instead of thinking about everything you need to do, focus on just the next step. Perhaps it's helping with morning routines or preparing a nutritious meal. Celebrate these small accomplishments. They're not insignificant; they're the building blocks of successful care and personal resilience.

Adapting routines may help. Consider how your usual routines might need to change to better serve you and your loved one. For instance, if your family member becomes distressed by vacuum noise, you might need to adjust your cleaning schedule. Perhaps arrange for help when your loved one is out of the house, or consider alternative cleaning methods that create less disruption.

Remember that activities you once managed easily might now pose challenges. If you've always preserved your own vegetables but find it difficult to monitor a pressure cooker while caregiving, it's okay to find alternatives.

Connecting with others on similar journeys can be a powerful way to build resilience. You might discover new coping strategies or practical tips that others have found helpful in their own experiences.

Tips for Cultivating Resilience:

1. Practice the "Three Good Things" exercise daily, writing down three positive experiences or accomplishments from your day.

2. Break down tasks into smaller, manageable steps and celebrate each small victory and progress made. Prioritize these, recognizing that it might not be possible to get them all done.

3. Embrace self-compassion during setbacks, treating yourself with kindness and understanding.

4. Reframe challenges as opportunities for growth and learning, asking yourself what you can learn from each experience.

5. Connect with others on similar journeys for support and shared wisdom.

6. Celebrate your victories, no matter how small, acknowledging moments of connection, progress, and joy.

7. Take time for self-reflection and self-care, engaging in activities that bring you joy, relaxation, and replenishment.

8. Lean on your faith and spiritual practices, engaging in prayer, meditation, or other practices that bring you peace and renewal.

When you take care of yourself and build your inner strength, you're better prepared to handle the good and challenging days of caregiving. Each day adds to your experience and understanding, even when things feel difficult. Remember that you're growing stronger and more capable, step by step, even if it doesn't always feel that way in the moment.

Chapter 15: Self-Reflection

Scripture: "Search me, O God, and know my heart." (Psalm 139:23a, KJV)

Caring for others often means running from task to task. But it's important to pause sometimes and check in with yourself. These quiet moments help you understand what you're feeling and what you need. Take comfort in knowing there's divine support for this inner work.

Devotional: Take time to look at your feelings and experiences with kindness and honesty. It's okay to notice what's challenging and what's going well. It's normal if looking inward is sometimes difficult—you're doing important work. When you pause to reflect, you might discover things you're proud of and areas where you need support.

As you open your heart to honest reflection, His loving presence helps you recognize both strength and areas for growth. Remember that in moments of self-reflection, you're never alone—God's compassionate presence guides your journey of discovery.

Prayer: *God, guide me into honest reflection with gentle wisdom. When self-examination is daunting, help me view myself through Your eyes of love. Grant me courage to explore shadows and light within my heart. In moments of doubt or self-judgment, remind me to extend the same compassion to myself that I offer others. Help me embrace growth and struggle as sacred parts of my journey. May my reflections* *deepen my capacity for authentic caregiving and self-awareness. When critical thoughts arise, grant me grace to respond with understanding. Let my growing self-knowledge strengthen my ability to care for others while honoring my own needs. In gratitude for this practice of sacred reflection, I rest in Your peace. Amen.*

Checking in with yourself helps you stay connected to who you are beyond your caregiving role.

Ask yourself: How am I really feeling today? What's working well? What's challenging? You might notice you've learned new skills or found strength you didn't expect. You might also realize when things feel too heavy and you need extra support.

Try spending just a few quiet minutes each day to tune into your thoughts and feelings. This simple practice can help you see more clearly what you need to keep going. Remember, understanding yourself better helps you be there for others in a more balanced way.

Take a moment now to appreciate how far you've come. Every new skill you've learned, every challenge you've faced—these are all part of your growth. When things feel difficult, this is also important to notice. It might be a signal that it's time to make some changes or reach out for help.

> **Challenge:** Finding time for self-reflection amidst the constant demands of caring for a loved one.

Solution: Create a daily "reflection ritual"—a designated time and space for introspection.

Example: Set aside 15 minutes each evening for self-reflection. Find a quiet spot, light a candle, and write in a journal about your day. Reflect on the moments that brought you joy, the challenges you faced, and the insights you gained. This ritual can help you process your experiences and emotions, providing a sense of closure and perspective at the end of each day.

Tips for Nurturing Self-Reflection:

1. Create a daily "reflection ritual." Set aside a designated time and space for introspection each day - make it part of the routine you establish for your loved one.

2. Use everyday moments for reflection. Integrate self-reflection into your daily routine by using everyday activities as prompts.

3. Engage in reflective journaling. Set aside a few minutes each day to write about your experiences, thoughts, and feelings.

4. Use tangible prompts for reflection. If memory or cognitive changes make self-reflection challenging, use concrete prompts like photos, music, or journal prompts to stimulate reflection.

5. Share reflections with trusted others. Engage in reflective conversations with care partners, family members, friends, therapists, or support groups.

6. Engage in creative self-reflection. Express your reflections through creative outlets like painting, poetry, music, or storytelling.

7. Practice self-compassion in reflection. Approach your self-reflection with kindness and understanding.

8. Use reflection to connect with your spiritual side. If spirituality is important to you, use moments of self-reflection to connect with your faith or sense of higher purpose.

Self-reflection is a personal practice that can take many forms. Try different approaches to find what works for you. Be patient and kind to yourself as you build this habit, trusting that consistent practice will deepen your self-understanding.

Chapter 16: Finding Joy

Scripture: "This is the day which the Lord hath made; we will rejoice and be glad in it." (Psalm 118:24, KJV)

God brings moments of joy into our daily caregiving. He knows that happiness gives us strength to keep caring well.

Devotional: Through God's help, you can find moments to smile and laugh, even during hard days. He shows you it's okay to feel happy while caregiving —joy doesn't mean you care any less. God understands when happiness feels far away, and helps you notice small moments worth celebrating. Trust that He gives you these bright moments to lift your spirit and renew your energy. When you let yourself enjoy good moments, His presence helps make them even brighter. Remember that finding joy in each day helps you and your loved one face challenges better.

Prayer: *God, help me see the enjoyable moments in each day. When things feel heavy, show me reasons to smile. Help me know it's okay to experience joy while caregiving. In busy times, remind me to pause and savor simple pleasures. Guide me to share happy moments with my loved one. When sadness comes, help me still find bits of joy. Let these happy times give me strength to keep caring well. Thank you for the gift of joy in everyday moments. Amen.*

It's good to feel happy while caring for someone—those moments help you keep going. Share a laugh, enjoy quiet time together, or just take in a peaceful moment. These bright spots make the hard days easier.

Take time to enjoy small pleasures, like your morning coffee or finishing a task. When these moments happen, let yourself experience that happiness. This helps you stay strong and positive.

Look for ways to share enjoyable activities with your loved one. Maybe it's looking at photos, listening to music, or sitting outside together. Focus on being together, not on doing things perfectly.

Remember: Happy moments, even small ones, help you and your loved one feel better. They give you energy to handle the challenges and make your time together more meaningful.

Challenge: Struggling with guilt or selfishness when experiencing joy while your loved one is suffering.

Solution: Know that your joy matters too. Happiness is not a zero-sum game—your moments of joy don't take away from your loved one, they add to the well-being of you both.

Example: When you catch yourself feeling guilty for laughing with a friend or enjoying a hobby, gently reframe your thinking. You might say to yourself, "My joy is not a betrayal. It's a resource that helps me be a better, more resilient care partner. When I nurture my happiness, I have more to give to my loved one."

Tips for Cultivating Joy:

1. Set a daily intention to notice moments of happiness. Each morning, make a conscious commitment to find instances of joy throughout the day.

2. Engage in meaningful activities that bring pleasure. Consider your loved one's interests, abilities, and sources of enjoyment. Adapt cherished hobbies or discover new ones that you can enjoy together.

3. Embrace laughter and playfulness. Give yourself permission to find humor and lightness, even amidst the challenges.

4. Create a "Joy Menu" or "Laughter Prescription." Write down a list of simple pleasures, funny memories, or amusing activities that consistently bring a smile.

5. Prioritize self-care and activities that nourish your own happiness. As a care partner, your joy matters, too.

6. Savor the simple sensory delights of daily life. Encourage your loved one to notice and appreciate the small sensory pleasures that can bring comfort and contentment.

7. Practice gratitude and celebrate the good. Make it a daily habit to reflect on the blessings and joys, no matter how small.

8. Be gentle with yourself on the tough days. Cultivating joy doesn't mean denying the hard emotions or striving for constant happiness.

Be patient with yourself and your loved one. There will be ups and downs, laughter and tears. Embrace the full spectrum of the experience, knowing that your ability to find and create joy is a remarkable strength. Trust that God is with you in every moment, bringing hope and happiness even in the middle of challenges.

Chapter 17: Coping with Grief and Loss

Scripture: "The Lord is nigh unto them that are of a broken heart." (Psalm 34:18a, KJV)

God remains close to you when your heart is heavy with grief. He understands the pain you feel as you navigate the changes and losses that come with caregiving.

Devotional: In times of sorrow, trust that God is near, offering comfort and strength. He sees the depth of your love and the weight of your grief. Allow yourself to lean into His presence, finding solace knowing He understands your pain. God's love is a balm for your broken heart, a reminder that you're not alone in your struggles. His nearness is a constant source of hope and healing.

Prayer: *God, I come to You with a heavy heart, burdened by the grief and loss that accompanies this caregiving journey. I trust in Your promise to be near to those who are brokenhearted. Help me feel Your comforting presence in my moments of sorrow. Remind me it's okay to acknowledge and express my pain, for it reflects the deep love I hold. When the weight of grief feels overwhelming, give me the strength to keep going, knowing that You are by my side. Help me find moments of peace and solace in Your unchanging love. Thank You for Your constant care and compassion, and for the hope that I find in You. Amen.*

Feeling grief while caregiving is natural and shows your deep love. It's okay to feel sad about changes and losses, whether they're small daily ones or bigger life changes. Your feelings are real and important. By accepting your grief while still caring for your loved one, you handle this journey more honestly. Remember that sharing your feelings with others who understand can help you cope better with loss.

In your role of supporting your loved one, you may experience a complex range of emotions, including grief. This grief can come in waves, triggered by changes in your loved one's abilities or shifts in your relationship. It's crucial to recognize and honor these feelings. Your grief is a testament to the depth of your love and the significance of your relationship. Consider creating a personal ritual or finding a special space where you can express and process your emotions.

Recognizing and honoring the full spectrum of your emotions is a crucial step. Sadness, anger, guilt, fear, and even moments of relief are all natural responses to the losses you're experiencing. Allow yourself to feel these emotions without judgment, understanding that they are a testament to the depth of your love and the significance of your relationship.

Challenge: Finding healthy ways to express and process complex emotions while managing caregiving responsibilities.

Solution: Create an "Emotion Journal" to track and process your feelings.

> **Example:** Set aside a few minutes each day to jot down your emotions in a dedicated notebook. You might write, "Today, I felt sad when Mom couldn't remember our favorite recipe, but I also felt grateful when she smiled at me during dinner." This practice helps validate your experiences and track your emotions over time.

As you move through the ebbs and flows of grief, self-compassion becomes an invaluable tool. Treat yourself with the same kindness and understanding you'd offer a dear friend facing similar challenges.

Tips for Coping with Grief and Loss:

1. Acknowledge and validate your emotions, recognizing that grief is a natural response to the losses you're experiencing.

2. Create a ritual or dedicated space for expressing and processing your feelings such as journaling, meditation, or spending time in nature.

3. Practice self-compassion, treating yourself with kindness and understanding as you grieve.

4. Join a support group to connect with others who understand your experiences.

5. Incorporate mindfulness exercises into your daily routine to help ground you in the present

moment and provide a respite from the intensity of grief.

6. Create a "Joy Jar" to capture and celebrate moments of happiness, connection, and gratitude.

7. Honor your loved one's life story through a "Living Legacy" project such as a scrapbook or video compilation, involving family and friends in the process.

8. Seek support from a therapist or counselor if you feel overwhelmed or need additional coping strategies.

9. Remember, your grief is a testament to the depth of your love and the significance of your relationship with your loved one.

10. Hold onto hope, knowing that even during grief and loss, you can still find moments of joy, connection, and love.

In the face of grief and loss, it's easy to feel overwhelmed and alone. But even in the darkest of moments, there is hope to be found in the nearness of God. He sees your broken heart and offers His comforting presence. Allow yourself to lean into His love, trusting that He will provide the strength and solace you need. Your grief is a reflection of your deep love, and God understands and honors that love.

Chapter 18: Embracing Change: Navigating emotions

Scripture: "Jesus Christ the same yesterday, and to day, and for ever." (Hebrews 13:8, KJV)

Admit life's constant changes, there is One who remains steadfast and unchanging—God. His love and presence are the anchors that hold you secure through every shifting circumstance.

Devotional: As you navigate the ever-changing landscape of caregiving, find comfort in the constancy of God. He is your firm foundation, the rock upon which you can stand when everything else seems to shift. In moments of uncertainty or fear, lean into His unchanging love. When you feel overwhelmed by the emotions that come with each new challenge, rest in the assurance that He is with you, just as He has always been. Trust that He will guide you through each transition with the same tender care and unwavering devotion He has always shown. As you embrace the changes in your journey, embrace also the unchanging truth of His love for you.

Prayer: *God, thank You for being the constant in my life, the same yesterday, today, and forever. When the changes and challenges of caregiving threaten to overwhelm me, help me cling to Your unchanging love. Remind me that no matter what I face, You are with me, offering Your strength, wisdom, and comfort. Help me trust in Your faithfulness, even when my emotions are swirling and my path feels uncertain. Give me the courage to embrace change, knowing* *that You are embracing me through it all. Help me extend grace to myself and to my loved one as we navigate this journey together. May Your constant presence be our anchor and our hope. Amen.*

Embracing change doesn't mean denying the difficult emotions that come with it—it means acknowledging them as natural responses to your evolving journey. Every feeling you experience is valid, from moments of frustration to glimpses of joy. Remember that navigating emotional changes takes patience, with your loved one and yourself. By honoring your feelings while remaining open to change, you create space for genuine connection and growth through each new season of caregiving.

You're likely to experience a complex range of emotions. You might feel love and compassion alongside frustration, sadness, or even guilt. When you notice strong emotions surfacing, take a moment to recognize them. Practice self-compassion by acknowledging the difficulty of your role. Embracing the changes in your life and relationship requires patience—not just with your loved one, but with yourself as well. It's okay to have bad days, and it's okay to celebrate the good ones.

It's important to recognize that the emotional landscape can be overwhelming at times. Care partners may experience a mix of grief, guilt, frustration, and exhaustion as they adapt to new responsibilities and witness the changes in their loved one.

Individuals adapting to cognitive changes may grapple with fear, anxiety, anger, and sadness. Acknowledging and honoring your emotions is a crucial step in embracing change and finding healthy ways to cope.

Challenge: You feel guilty taking time for yourself because you think you should only focus on your loved one's needs.

Solution: Reframe self-care as an essential part of being an effective care partner. Just as flight attendants advise you to put on your own oxygen mask before assisting others, caring for yourself allows you to bring your best self to the caregiving role.

Example: Schedule regular "self-care dates" in your calendar, treating them as non-negotiable commitments. Whether it's a coffee with friends, a yoga class, or a quiet walk in nature, prioritize activities that replenish your emotional reserves.

Tips for Embracing Change:

1. Acknowledge and validate your emotions as they arise, without judgment or self-criticism.

2. Practice mindfulness to stay grounded in the present moment and find pockets of peace.

3. Reframe your perspective to focus on the blessings and opportunities for growth amidst the challenges.

4. Prioritize self-care and seek support as a care partner, recognizing that your well-being is essential for providing compassionate care.

5. Explore new ways of communicating and engaging with the world, embracing non-verbal forms of expression and connection.

6. Find purpose and meaning in daily activities, no matter how small, to maintain a sense of identity and worth.

7. Practice self-compassion and be gentle with yourself, acknowledging that this path is not an easy one.

In the end, embracing change is about embracing the essence of life itself. It's about recognizing the destination does not define our journeys, but by the moments we share along the way. It's about finding the courage to let go of what was and open our hearts to what is. And it's about trusting that even in the face of great change, God's love remains the constant that guides us home.

You're held secure in a love that knows no bounds and, with each step, you're navigating this landscape with grace and resilience. And in the end, that is the most beautiful embrace of all.

CREATING A SUPPORTIVE ENVIRONMENT

Chapter 19: Celebrating Special Occasions

Scripture: "This is the day which the Lord hath made; we will rejoice and be glad in it." (Psalm 118:24, KJV)

Even in life's difficulties, God reminds us to find joy in each day and to celebrate the special moments He gives us. He invites us to rejoice in His goodness and to share that gladness with others.

Devotional: As you navigate the changes in your caregiving journey, trust that God is helping you find ways to make special days meaningful. He shows you that celebrations can still bring joy, even when they need to be adapted. Through His guidance, you discover simple gatherings can be just as significant as elaborate ones.

God gives you creativity to modify old traditions and establish new ones that better suit your current circumstances. When holidays or birthdays seem different from before, He helps you find fresh ways to honor these occasions. Trust that God is inspiring you with ideas to create special moments that matter, even if they look different than in the past. As you plan celebrations, sense His presence helping you make every moment count. Remember that marking special days, no matter how simply, keeps love and connection strong.

Prayer: *God, help me create celebrations that bring joy and meaning to our lives today. When old traditions need to change, show me new ways to make these days special. Grant me wisdom to plan activities that delight my loved one without causing stress. When celebrating is challenging, remind me that simple things can hold great significance. Help me cherish the memories of past celebrations while embracing the opportunity to make new ones. When my feelings are mixed about the changes in our traditions, help me maintain a positive perspective. May these special times draw us closer together and to You. Thank You for Your presence in every celebration. Amen.*

Special days don't need grand gestures to be meaningful. Finding new ways to celebrate that align with your loved one's current abilities helps everyone enjoy the moment. While traditions may change, the love behind them remains constant. By keeping celebrations simple and flexible, you create joyful memories that honor the present while cherishing the past.

As a care partner, you play a crucial role in adapting and facilitating special occasions. Focus on creating meaningful moments rather than elaborate events. Incorporate familiar elements, like music or foods, to evoke positive memories. These occasions offer you the opportunity to make new, joyful memories alongside treasured old ones. Even small gestures can make a day special and reinforce the bonds of love between you.

Together, you're discovering new ways to experience and create special moments. Celebrations provide chances to honor your loved one and the relationship you share. The key is to approach these events with flexibility, creativity, and an emphasis on what truly matters—your love and connection.

The most meaningful celebrations often come from simple, heartfelt gestures. A familiar song, a cherished photograph, or a favorite treat can spark joy and connection. By focusing on these moments of happiness and togetherness, you're reinforcing your bond and creating lasting, positive memories which enrich both your lives.

> **Challenge:** Balancing the desire to maintain past traditions with the need to adapt to current realities.
>
> **Solution:** Have an open, honest conversation with your loved one (if possible) and other family members about what aspects of the celebration are most important to everyone. Work together to find creative ways to honor the essence of those traditions in a manageable way.
>
> **Example:** "I know how much Dad has always loved our big Fourth of July barbecue. This year, instead of hosting everyone, what if we pack a special picnic lunch and take Dad to his favorite park? We can still have his favorite foods and spend quality time together, but in a way that feels more relaxed for everyone."

Tips for Making Special Occasions Meaningful:

1. Focus on simplicity and familiarity. Choose one or two key activities or rituals to focus on, such as a special meal or beloved holiday song.

2. Adapt celebrations to changing needs. Be flexible in adjusting the timing, duration, and activities to suit your loved one's energy levels and abilities.

3. Create a supportive environment. Keep gatherings small, choose familiar locations, and pay attention to comforting sensory details like soft lighting and gentle music.

4. Embrace the joy of the present moment. Focus on the delights of the current celebration, savoring the laughter, warmth, and sweetness of shared experiences.

5. Honor cherished memories through reminiscence. Look through photo albums together, share stories, and invite your loved one to share their favorite memories of past celebrations.

6. Create new traditions tailored to current abilities and interests. Embrace the opportunity to reimagine celebrations in a meaningful and manageable way.

7. Practice self-compassion and prioritize self-care. Recognize the emotional complexity of celebrating while caregiving and extend kindness to yourself.

8. Affirm the enduring power of love and connection. Recognize that your presence and participation are the most precious gifts, and trust that your loved one feels the love, even if they can't express it in traditional ways.

Celebrating special occasions is about adapting, not abandoning. It's about finding new ways to honor the essence of your traditions and the love that underlies them. Above all, remember that God is with you in every celebration, helping you find joy and meaning in each special moment.

Chapter 20: Finding Peace in Moments of Frustration

Scripture: "Come unto me, all ye that labour and are heavy laden, and I will give you rest." (Matthew 11:28, KJV)

In the challenges of caregiving, God offers His boundless peace. He invites you to come to Him when you feel weary and burdened, promising rest for your soul.

Devotional: God provides calm strength when patience feels thin. Through His wisdom, you discover ways to transform difficult moments into opportunities for grace. He gives you permission to acknowledge frustration while drawing from His well of peace, knowing that His presence can soothe troubled hearts. God understands when tasks become overwhelming, and offers His gentle comfort to both care partner and loved one.

Trust that He guides your responses in tense moments, helping you approach challenges with renewed patience. When you open your heart to His peace, His calming presence flows through your words and actions, helping you create an atmosphere of understanding. Remember that in moments of frustration, God's peace remains available, offering renewed strength and perspective for you and your loved one.

Prayer: *God, guide me through moments of frustration with Your calming presence. When patience wears thin, help me find renewed strength in Your peace. Grant me wisdom to respond with gentle understanding when tensions rise. When tasks become too much, remind me that Your peace is always available. Help me create an environment of calm support for my loved one. May my heart stay open to Your guidance in challenging moments. When frustrations mount, grant me grace to pause and seek Your peace. Let these difficult times draw me closer to Your loving presence. In gratitude for Your peace that surpasses understanding, I rest in You. Amen.*

Frustration is not a failure but an opportunity to practice peace-filled caregiving. Through acknowledging these challenging emotions while staying connected to God's peace, you develop greater patience and understanding. A calm presence and gentle responses can transform even the most frustrating moments. By approaching challenges with God's peace as your foundation, you create space for honest emotion and healing connection, discovering renewed strength for the journey ahead.

As a care partner, witnessing your loved one's frustration can be heart-wrenching. You play a crucial role in creating an environment of calm and support during these challenging moments. Your patience and understanding can be a powerful balm for their agitation.

Frustration is a shared experience, affecting your loved one living with the condition and you as their care partner. By approaching these moments together with patience and understanding, you can transform challenges into opportunities for connection and growth.

Consider creating a "frustration toolkit" together. This could include calming activities you both enjoy, like listening to favorite music, looking at family photos, or taking a short walk. When tensions rise, you can turn to these shared coping strategies, reinforcing your partnership in facing challenges.

Your loved one's anger or agitation is often a response to the situation, not a personal attack. Take a moment to breathe deeply and center yourself before responding with gentleness and empathy. Validate your loved one's feelings by saying something like, "I can see how frustrating this must be for you. Let's work through it together." This acknowledgment of their emotions can help diffuse tension and foster a sense of understanding.

When frustration levels rise, try incorporating a brief mindfulness exercise. Guide your loved one in taking a few slow, deep breaths, focusing on the sensation of the air moving in and out. This simple act of centering can help calm the mind and body, making it easier to approach the task with renewed patience.

It's also crucial to prioritize self-care and seek support when needed. Take moments throughout the day to practice deep breathing, stretch, or engage in activities that bring you joy and relaxation. Reach out to friends, family, or support groups who can offer a listening ear and words of encouragement.

Challenge: Feeling overwhelmed when your loved one's frustration leads to anger or agitation.

Solution: Take a moment to pause, breathe deeply, and silently pray or reflect before responding gently. Remind yourself that their anger is often a response to the situation, not directed at you personally.

Example: When your loved one starts to get agitated because she can't find her favorite sweater, try to step back and take a few deep breaths. Then, calmly approach her and say, "I understand how upsetting this must be. Let's look for your sweater together." By responding with empathy and understanding, you may be able to help your loved one feel more at ease.

Tips for Managing Frustration and Promoting Peaceful Interactions:

1. When your loved one becomes frustrated, take a moment to pause and breathe deeply before responding. This brief self-care practice can help you approach the situation with a calm, centered presence.

2. Validate your loved one's feelings of frustration, even if you don't fully understand the cause. Use phrases like, "I can see how challenging this is for you right now," or "It's okay to feel frustrated when things aren't going as planned."

3. Break tasks or activities into smaller, more manageable steps. Guide them through the

process one item at a time, offering simple, clear instructions.

4. Focus on celebrating your loved one's efforts and engagement, rather than the end result. Offer praise for their participation and perseverance.

5. If a task becomes too challenging or frustrating, gently redirect your loved one's attention to a more manageable or enjoyable activity.

6. Practice self-compassion and patience with yourself when feelings of frustration arise. Remind yourself that you're doing the best you can in a challenging situation.

7. Incorporate moments of mindfulness and stress-relief into your daily routine such as deep breathing exercises, meditation, prayer, or engaging in a favorite hobby.

8. Seek support from others who understand the challenges. Join a care partner support group, talk with a trusted friend or counselor, or turn to your faith community for encouragement and guidance.

Managing frustration is an ongoing practice, not a one-time achievement. Be patient and compassionate with yourself and your loved one.

Chapter 21: Adapting Your Home

Scripture: "For he shall give his angels charge over thee, to keep thee in all thy ways." (Psalm 91:11, KJV)

God surrounds you with His divine protection and guidance as you navigate the challenges of caregiving. He promises to send His angels to watch over you and your loved one, ensuring your safety and well-being in every aspect of your journey.

Devotional: As you adapt your home to meet the changing needs of your loved one, trust that God is directing your efforts with His loving wisdom. He understands the importance of creating a safe and comforting environment, and He sends His angels to guide your decisions and actions. These heavenly messengers keep you both secure in all your ways, from the physical modifications you make to the emotional support you provide. As you work to transform your living space into a haven of care and protection, know that God's angels are alongside you, strengthening your hands and inspiring your heart. Their presence fills each room with divine peace and assurance, reminding you that you're never alone in your caregiving journey.

Prayer: *God, thank You for the promise of Your angelic protection as I navigate the challenges of caregiving. I trust You are sending Your heavenly messengers to guide and guard us in all our ways, especially as I work to adapt our home to meet my loved one's changing needs. Grant me wisdom and* *discernment as I make decisions about modifications and safety measures. Help me create a space that reflects Your love and care, where my loved one can feel secure, comfortable, and valued. Give me strength and patience as I implement these changes, and remind me that Your angels are always nearby, ready to assist and encourage me. May our home become a sanctuary of Your peace and presence, a place where we can both rest in the assurance of Your unfailing love and protection. Amen.*

Creating a supportive home environment is a profound expression of care that honors safety and dignity. Through thoughtful modifications and adaptations, you build spaces that nurture independence while ensuring security. While some changes may seem significant, remember that each change serves to create a sanctuary of comfort and support. By approaching home adaptations with practical wisdom and loving intention, you transform your living space into a haven that promotes well-being.

As you consider making adaptations, focus on areas where safety and ease of use are most important, like the bathroom and kitchen. Installing features such as non-slip mats, a shower chair, or safety locks on appliances can significantly reduce the risk of accidents. It may be time to install an alarm that will alert you if your loved one leaves bed during the night, or to put an alarm on the house doors if wandering is an issue.

While planning these changes, try to balance safety with maintaining a sense of normalcy and dignity for your loved one. Involve them in decisions when possible, and explain changes in a positive, supportive manner. A well-adapted home environment can make your caregiving tasks easier and less stressful as well.

Start by assessing the home from your loved one's perspective, looking for potential hazards and areas that may cause confusion or frustration. Remove tripping risks, ensure walkways are clear and well-lit, and install handrails and grab bars in key areas to provide added stability and support.

To reduce confusion and assist with orientation, incorporate visual cues and memory aids throughout the home. Hang a large, easy-to-read calendar and clock, and label cupboards, drawers, and doors with simple words or pictures that show their contents and purpose.

Create a soothing, calming atmosphere by choosing decor and furnishings that promote relaxation and familiarity. Use calming colors, incorporate cozy textures, and display cherished photos and mementos that evoke happy memories and provide a sense of connection to the past.

As you make these modifications, involve your loved one in the process as much as possible. Ask for their input on color choices, furniture arrangements, and decor preferences. Honoring their opinions and involving them in decision-making can help promote a sense of control and autonomy. You may find that what you leave in place is as important as what you change. Maybe your loved one has a favorite chair that has been in the same place for years.

Remember, adapting your home is an ongoing process that may require adjustments over time. Be open to making additional modifications as needs change.

Tips for Adapting Your Home:

1. Conduct a thorough assessment from your loved one's perspective, making a list of areas that need attention.

2. Prioritize safety modifications, focusing on high-risk areas like the bathroom and kitchen.

3. Enhance navigation and orientation using clear visual cues, labels, and easy-to-read clocks.

4. Create a calming atmosphere with soothing colors, comfortable furnishings, and familiar objects.

5. Adapt spaces and tasks to support continued participation in daily activities and promote independence.

6. Incorporate assistive technologies, such as motion-sensor lights or medication reminders, to enhance safety and independence.

7. Consult with occupational therapists or dementia care specialists for personalized recommendations tailored to your situation.

8. Involve your loved one in the modification process, honoring their opinions and promoting a sense of control and autonomy.

As you work to create a supportive environment, take a moment to pause and connect with your intentions. Visualize your loved one moving through the space, feeling a sense of comfort, safety, and belonging. Hold this image in your mind, allowing it to guide your efforts and infuse each adaptation with love and purpose.

Transforming your home is an ongoing process of love and dedication. Each thoughtful modification contributes to a safer, more comfortable environment that honors the dignity and needs of your loved one.

NURTURING RELATIONSHIPS AND CONNECTIONS

Chapter 22: Nurturing Relationships

Scripture: "A friend loveth at all times, and a brother is born for adversity." (Proverbs 17:17, KJV)

Sharing a laugh with friends, enjoying moments with family, or connecting with other care partners gives you strength to keep going. While some days feel overwhelming, these relationships help lighten your load. When you nurture these connections, even briefly, you create a support system that makes caregiving more manageable.

God provides these relationships as gifts. Through phone calls, visits, or even quick text messages, these connections remind you that you're not alone. Every small interaction can bring comfort and renewed energy for your daily responsibilities.

Devotional: In the changing patterns of connection, God provides new ways to express and experience love. Through His wisdom, you discover that bonds of the heart remain strong even when other aspects of relationship shift. He gives you creativity to find fresh ways of connecting, knowing that love speaks through more than words. God understands when relationships face challenges, and guides you toward meaningful moments of connection. Trust that He helps you nurture old and new bonds, offering support through the presence of others. When you open your heart to different forms of connection, His love flows through every interaction, helping you maintain precious relationships.

Prayer: *God, guide me in nurturing the relationships You've blessed me with. When connections feel strained, help me find new ways to express love and care. Grant me patience to adapt to changing patterns of interaction. In times of loneliness, remind me of the support system You've provided. Help me maintain meaningful connections with my loved one and others. May my heart stay open to different ways of expressing and receiving love. When communication becomes challenging, grant me wisdom to connect through presence. Let these relationships continue to grow and strengthen through Your grace. In gratitude for the gift of connection, I rest in peace. Amen.*

As your loved one's needs change, you'll discover new ways to show love and stay connected. Trust that God guides you in finding these new paths of connection, helping you adapt while keeping your relationships strong and meaningful.

> **Challenge:** You miss a friend who hasn't called in a while and wonder why they're not reaching out, leading to feelings of disconnection and loneliness.
>
> **Solution:** Take the initiative to reach out instead of waiting. Remember that friends may have their own challenges or might be unsure how to help. A simple call or

message can rebuild connection and provide the support you need.

Example: When you notice it's been weeks since hearing from a close friend, resist assuming they don't want to talk. Instead, pick up the phone and make that call. Often you'll discover they've been dealing with their own struggles or weren't sure how to support you. This simple act of reaching out can renew your friendship and provide both of you with needed connection and support.

Maintaining relationships with your broader social circle is equally important. Friends and family members may distance themselves, unsure of how to interact or offer support. Educate your social circle and provide specific ways they can help and interact.

It's crucial to prioritize your own relationships outside of your caregiving role. Your well-being directly impacts the quality of care you can provide. Use technology for quick check-ins with friends, join a care partner support group, or schedule regular respite care to allow time for personal connections.

Tips for Nurturing Connections:

1. Create Meaningful Rituals: Establish simple, regular routines that you can do together such as a daily walk or a special mealtime ritual.

2. Embrace Non-Verbal Communication: Use gentle touch, eye contact, and facial expressions to convey love and support.

3. Practice Mindful Presence: Learn to be fully present in each moment you share, setting aside worries and focusing on the here and now.

4. Engage Multiple Senses: Plan activities that stimulate various senses, such as gardening, baking, or giving hand massages.

5. Adapt Activities to Abilities: Modify favorite activities to match your loved one's current abilities, maintaining a sense of accomplishment and shared enjoyment.

6. Use Validation Techniques: Acknowledge and affirm your loved one's feelings, even if their perception of reality differs from yours.

7. Create a Memory Box: Fill a special box with items that hold significance for your loved one to spark conversations and shared moments of reminiscence.

8. Leverage User-Friendly Technology: Explore simple tech options to maintain connections with family and friends who can't visit often.

9. Join Community Activities Together: Participate in events designed for people dealing with cognitive changes and their care partners.

10. Educate and Involve Others: Help friends and family understand the diagnosis and provide specific ways they can interact and offer support.

Nurturing relationships is not always easy, but it is always worthwhile. It reminds us of the enduring power of human connection, even in the face of cognitive decline, and of the love that continues to bind us together, transcending the limitations of memory or recognition.

Lean on your support network, seek out resources and guidance, and prioritize your own self-care. By nurturing your relationships—with your loved one, with others, and with yourself—you're creating a foundation of love and resilience that will carry you through the challenges. Trust that God is guiding you in this sacred work, strengthening your bonds and filling your connections with His gracious love.

Chapter 23: Setting Boundaries

Scripture: "Let your moderation be known unto all men." (Philippians 4:5a, KJV)

God calls us to live with balance and moderation in all things, including our caregiving roles. He understands the importance of setting healthy boundaries that allow us to care for others while also tending to our own needs. Setting healthy limits helps you care better. These boundaries help you stay well and give your best to your loved one.

Devotional: God's wisdom teaches us that good care requires good boundaries. He knows that as caregivers, we need rest and support to continue serving others effectively. God helps us understand that it's okay to communicate our needs, take breaks, and ask for help when we are overloaded. He gently reminds us we cannot pour from an empty cup and, that by taking care of ourselves, we are better equipped to care for those we love.

As we lean on Him for strength and discernment, He helps us find the right balance between giving of ourselves and respecting our own limits. Trust that as you seek to honor God through your caregiving journey, He will guide you in setting boundaries that allow you to serve with a heart full of love and compassion.

Prayer: *God, grant me the wisdom and courage to set healthy boundaries in my caregiving role. Help me remember that taking care of myself is a necessary* *part of being able to care for others effectively. When I experience guilt about setting limits or taking time for myself, remind me that You have called me to live with balance and moderation. Give me discernment to know when to say "yes" and when to say "no," and the strength to communicate my needs with kindness and clarity. Help me trust that by taking care of myself physically, emotionally, and spiritually, I am honoring You and the responsibilities You have entrusted to me. Guide me in finding the right balance between giving of myself and respecting my own limits so that I may continue to serve with a heart full of love and compassion. Thank You for Your constant presence and support on this caregiving journey. Amen.*

Think of boundaries as guardrails that protect you and your loved one, not walls that keep people out. These limits ensure you can keep caring well over the long run. You don't have to be available every minute of every day. Work with family members or other helpers to schedule regular breaks. Maybe someone else can take the evening shift or a weekend morning. When you return refreshed, you'll have more energy and patience for caregiving.

> **Challenge:** You feel guilty for taking personal time away from your caregiving duties.
>
> **Solution:** Establish a regular "self-care" schedule and communicate it clearly to family members and your loved one.

Example: Set aside every Wednesday afternoon for a yoga class and coffee with friends. Arrange for a family member or respite care to cover this time each week, making it a non-negotiable part of your routine.

Tips for Setting Boundaries:

1. Communicate clearly and kindly: Use "I" statements to express your needs and limits while also acknowledging the needs of your loved one and other family members.

2. Be specific: Clearly define your boundaries, such as the times you're available for caregiving tasks or the types of tasks you're willing to take on.

3. Prioritize self-care: Make time for activities that recharge and rejuvenate you such as hobbies, exercise, or social activities.

4. Seek support: Don't hesitate to ask for help from family members, friends, or professional services when needed.

5. Be flexible: Recognize that boundaries may need to be adjusted over time as circumstances change.

Setting boundaries shows love for yourself and your loved one. These limits help you stay strong and balanced so you can keep giving good care over the long run. Think of boundaries as your foundation for sustainable caregiving, not as barriers.

When you take care of your own needs alongside your loved one's, you create a healthier situation for everyone. Your well-being matters too. By setting clear, caring limits, you'll have more energy and patience for the journey ahead.

Chapter 24: Leaving a Legacy

Scripture: "The memory of the just is blessed." (Proverbs 10:7, KJV)

Our memories and life stories matter deeply. Each shared experience, family tradition, and special moment helps build a meaningful legacy. By preserving these memories, we keep important connections alive and pass on what matters most.

Devotional: Through God's wisdom, we learn that keeping memories alive brings comfort and joy. He shows us ways to remember the good times and important stories that have shaped our lives and the lives of our loved ones. God understands the deep significance of these memories and helps us find meaningful ways to preserve them. As we trust in His guidance, He leads us to collect and share the stories that matter most, ensuring that they stay alive for generations to come. When we work to save these memories, His love imbues them with even greater meaning and purpose. Remember every story you save is precious to God and serves as a testament to His faithfulness in your family's journey.

Prayer: *God, guide me as I strive to preserve the important memories and stories that my loved one and I have shared. When memories start to fade, show me creative and effective ways to keep them alive. Help me be attentive to the special moments worth remembering and documenting. As we share these stories together, remind me of Your deep care for each and every one of them. Give me the wisdom* *and perseverance to save these memories so that others can know them, too. When the task of preserving memories feels overwhelming, help me take it one story at a time, trusting in Your strength. May these saved stories help our family stay connected and grounded in what truly matters. Thank You for being an integral part of our life stories and legacies. Amen.*

As a care partner, you have a unique opportunity to help preserve and celebrate the life story of your loved one. Embracing storytelling can be a profound way to honor their experiences and the love you share. This might involve helping them recall and share memories, documenting their life story, or creating memory books together. Remember, you're not just a care partner; you're a keeper of memories, a storyteller, and a crucial link in passing on your loved one's legacy. Often, even someone who can't remember what they had for breakfast can remember the names of their childhood teachers, what their father did for a living, or where they used to go on summer vacations.

Together, you're on a journey of preserving memories and creating a lasting legacy. This process is about more than just recalling past events; it's about celebrating a life lived, acknowledging the impact one person can have on the world, and strengthening the bonds between you. For the person experiencing memory changes, sharing their story allows them to reaffirm their identity and the value of their life experiences. Participating in this storytelling process deepens your understanding and appreciation of your loved one's life.

Engaging in this legacy-building process can take many forms. You might spend time looking through old photographs together, recording oral histories, or creating a memory box filled with significant objects. These activities not only help preserve memories but also provide meaningful ways to spend time together, fostering moments of connection and joy.

Leaving a legacy isn't just about grand achievements; it's also about the small moments, the everyday kindnesses, and the love shared between people. By focusing on these stories and memories, you're creating a legacy of enduring love that will continue to inspire and comfort long into the future.

One of the most powerful ways to celebrate a life story is through storytelling. Sharing memories, both joyful and challenging, can be a profound source of connection and healing. It's an opportunity to deepen your understanding of your loved one, to see them beyond the lens of cognitive changes, and to recall the fullness of their life.

> **Challenge:** Feeling overwhelmed by the task of capturing and preserving a loved one's life story while managing the daily demands of caregiving.
>
> **Solution:** Start small and focus on one story, one memory at a time. Enlist the help of family and friends to share the responsibility and joy of legacy building.
>
> **Example:** Set a goal to write one cherished memory of your loved one each week. Invite other family

members to do the same. Over time, these small acts of remembrance will grow into a beautiful tribute to your loved one's life.

Tips for Celebrating Life Stories and Creating a Lasting Legacy:

1. Start a Memory Journal: Keep a journal to record stories, memories, and reflections. This can be a collaborative effort among family members.

2. Create a Life Story Book: Compile photographs, mementos, and written anecdotes into a book that tells the story of your loved one's life.

3. Use Technology: Record audio or video interviews to capture stories in the person's own voice. These recordings can become treasured family heirlooms.

4. Engage in Reminiscence Activities: Use prompts like music, old photographs, or familiar objects to spark memories and encourage storytelling.

5. Involve Family and Friends: Invite others to contribute their memories and stories, creating a richer, more diverse narrative of your loved one's life.

6. Focus on Sensory Memories: Don't just rely on words. Incorporate favorite foods, scents, or

textures that can trigger positive memories and associations.

7. Create a Memory Box: Fill a special box with meaningful objects that represent different aspects of your loved one's life and experiences.

8. Write Letters to Future Generations: Encourage your loved one to write letters sharing wisdom, advice, or love to younger family members or future generations.

9. Celebrate Small Moments: Legacy isn't just about big achievements. Record and celebrate the everyday moments that define a life well-lived.

10. Engage in Legacy Projects: Work together on projects that leave a tangible legacy, such as planting a garden, creating artwork, or contributing to a cause that's meaningful to your loved one.

The greatest legacy of all is the love you share, the compassion you offer, and the lives you touch along the way. In every act of kindness, every moment of connection, you're building a legacy that will endure long after memories fade.

Together, as you engage in the process of storytelling and memory-sharing, you're not just preserving the past—you're creating new memories and strengthening your bond in the present. You're weaving together a tapestry of experiences, wisdom, and love that will continue to inspire and comfort for generations to come, all while honoring the sacred story that God has written in your lives.

MANAGING BEHAVIORS AND CHANGES

Chapter 25: Honoring Emotions

Scripture: "A merry heart doeth good like a medicine." (Proverbs 17:22a, KJV)

God created us with a wide range of emotions, and He understands the powerful impact they can have on our well-being. In the midst of the caregiving journey, He reminds us that honoring and nurturing positive emotions can bring healing and joy.

Devotional: God, in His infinite wisdom, has gifted us with the capacity to experience and express emotions. He knows that a cheerful heart can be as powerful as medicine, lifting our spirits and bringing comfort in times of difficulty. As we navigate the challenges of caregiving, God gently guides us to create moments of joy, laughter, and emotional connection. He helps us understand that by validating and honoring the feelings of our loved ones, we create a safe space for them to express themselves freely. God also reminds us to tend to our own emotional well-being, knowing that having a merry heart better equips you to provide compassionate care. As we bring joy and emotional healing to others, we can remember that God is the ultimate source of comfort and peace.

Prayer: *God, thank You for the gift of emotions and the power they hold to bring healing and joy. As I care for my loved one, help me create moments of laughter, happiness, and heartfelt connection. Give* *me the wisdom and patience to validate and honor their feelings, even when they may not align with my perspective. Remind me to take care of my own emotional well-being, seeking out moments of joy and peace that will replenish my spirit. When the challenges of caregiving weigh heavily on my heart, help me remember that a cheerful heart is medicine. May I draw strength from Your infinite love and compassion, and may I be a channel of Your joy and comfort to those in my care. Amen.*

You play a crucial role in creating a supportive emotional environment for your loved one. Validating their feelings, even when their perception differs from reality, is a powerful tool in your caregiving toolkit. It requires patience, empathy, and sometimes, a shift in your own perspective.

You may face moments of confusion or frustration when your loved one's emotional reactions don't align with what you see as the current reality. It's challenging to balance addressing their immediate emotional needs with the practical aspects of care. By focusing on the feelings behind their words, you're providing essential emotional support.

Practice active listening and empathetic responses. When your loved one expresses fear, sadness, or any other emotion, acknowledge it openly. Simple phrases like, "I can see this is upsetting for you" or "It sounds like you're feeling anxious about this" can make a world of difference.

While supporting your loved one emotionally, don't forget to tend to your own emotional needs. Caregiving can be emotionally taxing, and your feelings are just as important. Seek support, take breaks when needed, and practice self-compassion.

Emotional validation is a bridge that can strengthen your connection, even as progressive symptoms bring changes to your relationship. By focusing on understanding and acknowledging each other's feelings, you create a space of mutual respect and support.

Try creating a daily check-in ritual where each of you share one feeling or experience from your day. This simple practice can enhance emotional awareness and provide opportunities for validation and support. It's not about solving problems, but about listening and acknowledging each other's experiences.

By prioritizing emotional validation in your interactions, you're nurturing a relationship built on empathy and understanding. This approach can reduce stress, strengthen your bond, and improve your quality of life. As you face the challenges together, your ability to validate and support each other emotionally will be a source of comfort and resilience.

Challenge: You feel exhausted and find it hard to consistently validate your loved one when their expressions of emotion become repetitive or continuous.

Solution: Develop some self-care strategies that allow you to replenish your emotional reserves. This might include taking short breaks when possible, practicing deep breathing or silent prayer during challenging moments, or creating your own support system for encouragement and respite.

Example: When your loved one repeats the same concerns over and over, take a deep breath before responding. If you feel your frustration growing, you might say, "I hear how worried you are. Let's sit together and listen to your favorite music for a few minutes."

Tips for Honoring Emotions and Creating Connection:

1. Acknowledge and validate feelings, even if they don't align with reality.

2. Respond to the emotion, not just the words.

3. Use nonverbal cues to convey empathy and support.

4. Practice patience and flexibility in your validation approach.

5. Know when to validate and when to redirect or distract.

6. Create a safe, compassionate space for all emotions to be expressed.

7. Validate your own emotions as a care partner.

8. Lean on your faith as a source of strength and guidance.

Remember, as you seek to bring joy and emotional healing to your loved one, God is with you every step of the way. He is the ultimate source of comfort, peace, and merry hearts. Trust in His guidance as you navigate the challenges of caregiving, and know that your efforts to honor emotions and create connection reflect His love and compassion.

Chapter 26: Meeting Your Loved One in Their Reality

Scripture: "Let nothing be done through strife or vainglory; but in lowliness of mind let each esteem other better than themselves." (Philippians 2:3, KJV)

God calls us to approach others with humility and to value their perspective above our own. This means meeting our loved ones in their reality, even when it differs from our own understanding.

Devotional: As we navigate the challenges of caregiving, God reminds us that love and understanding should be our guiding principles. When our loved one's perception of reality differs from ours, He calls us to respond with empathy and compassion rather than strife or pride. God gives us the grace to step into their world, to validate their emotions, and to create moments of connection that transcend the boundaries of shared reality. As we lean on His wisdom and strength, we discover that meeting our loved one in their reality is an act of sacred service, a way of honoring the inherent dignity and worth of the person entrusted to our care.

Prayer: *God, grant me the humility and grace to meet my loved one in their reality, even when it differs from my own. Help me lay aside any pride or desire to be right, and instead to approach our interactions with a heart of compassion and understanding. Give me the patience to listen attentively, the wisdom to validate their emotions, and the creativity to find ways* *to connect that brings joy and comfort. When I am tempted to correct or redirect, remind me love is more powerful than facts. May my words and actions always convey the deep respect and value I hold for my loved one. Thank You for the privilege of serving as a care partner, and for the opportunity to be a vessel of Your love and grace. Amen.*

You can create a safe and supportive environment by meeting your loved one in their reality. This approach requires flexibility, empathy, and sometimes, a willingness to step outside your own perception of the current situation.

You may find yourself in moments where your loved one's understanding of reality differs significantly from yours. It can be tempting to correct or redirect them to what you see as the truth. However, joining them in their reality often provides more comfort and reduces anxiety for both of you.

Practice validating their feelings and experiences, even when they don't align with your understanding of the present. Phrases like "I can see why that would make you feel that way" or "That sounds important to you" can help your loved one feel heard and understood.

Meeting each other in moments of differing realities is an opportunity to deepen your connection and understanding. Recognize that many factors influence subjective reality, including memories, emotions, and cognitive changes. By focusing on the feelings and needs behind the words or actions, rather than the factual accuracy, you can maintain a strong emotional connection even when perceptions differ.

When your loved one's perception of reality differs from yours, focus on the emotional truth rather than the factual details. Ask yourself, "What is the feeling behind their words, and how can I validate and respond to that emotion?"

Engage not only their mind but also their senses when connecting with your loved one. Sensory experiences like listening to familiar music, looking through old photos, or enjoying a favorite scent can help bridge the gap between past and present, creating moments of joy and familiarity.

> **Challenge:** Feeling frustrated or saddened when your loved one's perception of reality differs significantly from your own, leading to confusion or misunderstandings.
>
> **Solution:** Remind yourself that their experience is real to them, even if it doesn't align with the present moment. Focus on validating their emotions rather than correcting their understanding of reality.
>
> **Example:** If your loved one insists that someone needs to be picked up from school, even though that person is grown and lives elsewhere, take a deep breath and say, "I understand how much you want to see them and make sure they're okay. Let's look at some photos of their last visit and the special times you've shared

together." By acknowledging their feelings and redirecting the conversation to a related, positive memory, you can help them feel understood and supported.

Tips for meeting your loved one in their reality:

1. Embrace your loved one's perception of reality, even if it differs from your own.

2. Focus on the emotional truth behind your loved one's words and actions, rather than dwelling on factual details.

3. Simplify your communication style to accommodate your loved one's changing needs.

4. Engage your loved one's senses when connecting with them.

5. Be patient and compassionate with yourself as you adapt to the changes in your loved one's perception of reality.

6. Practice mindfulness when struggling to meet your loved one in their reality.

7. Remember that your acts of love, patience, and understanding are a testament to the depth of your devotion.

8. Lean on your support system.

As you continue to walk this path with your loved one, hold fast to the truth that love is the universal language that transcends all barriers. Your willingness to meet your loved one in their reality, with humility, compassion, and understanding, creates a sacred space where connection and joy can flourish, even amidst the challenges. Trust that God sees and honors your acts of selfless service, and that He will provide the strength and grace you need for each step of the journey.

Chapter 27: Addressing Behavioral Changes

Scripture: "A soft answer turneth away wrath: but grievous words stir up anger."(Proverbs 15:1, KJV)

God's wisdom teaches us that the way we respond to challenging situations can either bring peace or escalate tension. This means approaching behavioral changes with gentleness, patience, and understanding.

While Chapter 3 described the context of behavior, this chapter focuses on approaches for practical day-to-day solutions. Chapter 31 addresses the spiritual aspects of responding with compassion.

Devotional: As we navigate the complexities of changing behaviors, God reminds us that our words and actions have the power to soothe or agitate. A soft answer, filled with compassion and grace, can diffuse even the most difficult moments. When we feel frustrated or overwhelmed by our loved one's actions, God invites us to pause, seek His guidance, and respond with a heart of kindness. He gives us the wisdom to look beyond the surface, to recognize the unmet needs or emotions driving the behavior, and to address them with tenderness. As we rely on His strength and follow His example of gentle leadership, we create a nurturing atmosphere of peace and understanding.

Prayer: *God, grant me the patience and wisdom to address behavioral changes with a soft answer. When challenges arise and tensions threaten to* *escalate, help me pause and seek Your guidance. Give me the insight to look beyond the surface, to recognize the underlying needs or emotions driving the behavior, and to respond with compassion. May I speak and act with Your grace, bringing peace and comfort to even the most difficult situations. Help me create an atmosphere of gentleness and understanding, where my loved one feels safe, valued, and supported. When I feel overwhelmed or frustrated, remind me to turn to You for strength and wisdom. May I follow Your example of love and patience in every interaction. Amen.*

Witnessing behavioral changes in your loved one can be challenging and sometimes distressing. It can trigger fear about the future. It's important to approach these changes with patience and understanding, recognizing that they are often a form of communication rather than intentional difficult behavior.

You may encounter situations where your loved one becomes agitated, wanders, or experiences changes in sleep patterns. These behaviors can be exhausting and confusing, but they often stem from your loved one's changed perception of the world around them.

Learning to identify triggers for these behaviors is crucial. Pay attention to patterns—does agitation occur at certain times of day or in specific environments? By understanding these triggers, you can often prevent or minimize challenging situations before they escalate.

Creating a supportive environment is key. This might involve simplifying routines, reducing noise and clutter, or ensuring consistent sleep patterns. Your calm and reassuring presence can make a significant difference in managing these behavioral changes.

Recognize that behind every behavior is a need or emotion trying to be expressed. It might be discomfort, fear, or confusion. Acknowledging these underlying feelings can foster empathy and guide more effective responses.

Consider creating a “comfort plan” together during calm moments. This could include favorite activities, soothing music, or specific phrases that help during times of stress. Having these strategies ready can provide reassurance and structure when challenging behaviors arise.

As you face these behavioral changes together, focus on the emotional connection between you. Sometimes, simply being present and offering reassurance can be more powerful than any specific intervention. Your shared history and bond provide a foundation of trust and understanding that can help navigate even the most challenging situations.

Challenge: When your loved one becomes increasingly agitated and combative during personal care routines, you find yourself becoming frustrated and responding more sharply than you’d like.

Solution: Practice the "pause and respond" method - take a deep breath, remind yourself that the behavior stems from their condition, not defiance, and approach the situation with a gentle, calming presence. Break tasks into smaller steps and use positive, reassuring communication.

Example: Your loved one becomes agitated while helping them get dressed in the morning, pushing your hands away and becoming verbally upset. Instead of rushing to complete the task, pause and say softly, "I see this is difficult right now. Would you like to choose which arm to put through the sleeve first?" This gentle approach, combined with giving them some control over the process, often helps calm the situation and allows you to complete the task together more peacefully.

Tips for addressing behavioral changes:

1. Identify triggers: Keep a journal to track the timing, location, and potential precipitating factors of challenging behaviors.

2. Create a supportive environment: Simplify living spaces, establish consistent routines, and incorporate meaningful activities.

3. Use redirection and validation: Acknowledge concerns while gently redirecting attention to a positive activity or topic.

4. Prioritize safety: Ensure a safe environment by installing alarms, using identification bracelets, or creating enclosed areas for wandering.

5. Remain calm and reassuring: In moments of agitation or aggression, use a soothing voice and provide reassurance.

6. Establish consistent routines: Create a predictable daily schedule, including regular meal times, activities, and rest periods.

7. Seek support: Reach out to family, friends, or professional respite services for assistance. Attend support groups or educational programs.

8. Prioritize self-care: Make time for rest, nourishment, and personal pursuits. Engage in activities that bring you joy and relaxation.

Remember, every individual deserves to be treated with dignity, respect, and compassion. By approaching each day with a soft answer, patience, and a willingness to adapt, you can create a supportive environment that nurtures the spirit and honors the needs of every person involved. Trust that God is with you, guiding your words and actions with His wisdom and grace.

Chapter 28: Navigating Sundowning

Scripture: "He shall cover thee with his feathers, and under his wings shalt thou trust: his truth shall be thy shield and buckler. Thou shalt not be afraid for the terror by night; nor for the arrow that flieth by day." (Psalm 91:4-5, KJV)

In moments of sundowning, when confusion and fear intensify, God's love and protection are constant. He offers shelter and comfort, reassuring us we need not be afraid of the challenges that arise as day turns to night.

Devotional: As we navigate the complexities of sundowning, God reminds us He is our refuge and strength. When confusion and worry heighten at sunset, He covers us with His wings, providing a safe haven amidst the storm. Through His guidance, we discover ways to bring calm and peace to the evening hours, establishing routines that offer structure and reassurance. God understands the added stress that sundowning can bring, and He extends His patience and wisdom. As we turn to Him during these challenging times, His truth becomes our shield, helping us to create an atmosphere of tranquility and trust. Remember that even in the darkest of nights, God's presence brings light and hope, helping each of you feel safer and steadier in His unwavering love.

Prayer: *God, I come to You seeking strength and guidance as I navigate the challenges of sundowning. When confusion and agitation arise in the evening* *hours, help me to remember You are our constant source of comfort and protection. Grant me the patience and wisdom to create calming routines and peaceful environments that ease the transition from day to night. In moments when I feel overwhelmed or weary, renew my spirit with Your grace, reminding me You are always present, offering shelter and support. Help me trust in Your unfailing love, knowing that Your truth is a shield against fear and uncertainty. May Your peace fill our hearts and home, bringing light and hope to every evening. Thank You for Your constant care and provision, and for the assurance that we rest securely under the shelter of Your wings. Amen.*

As you care for your loved one, navigating the challenges of sundowning requires patience, creativity, and a deep well of compassion. Recognize that your loved one's increased confusion or agitation in the evening isn't intentional, but rather a symptom of changes to the brain's ability to process changing environments and routines. Your understanding and calm approach can make a significant difference in managing these symptoms.

Establishing a soothing evening routine can help signal to your loved one that it's time to wind down. This might include dimming lights gradually, playing soft music, or engaging in quiet activities together. Pay attention to environmental factors that might contribute to agitation, such as shadows, noise, or disruptions to their usual schedule.

Experiment with different activities that might help during sundowning periods. This could be gentle exercises, looking at memory books, or engaging in simple, repetitive tasks that provide a sense of purpose and calm. The key is to find what works best for your situation and be willing to adapt as needs change.

As you face these evening challenges together, let your shared history and bond guide your interactions. Sometimes, simply being present with each other, offering reassurance through touch or gentle words, can be the most powerful way to find light in the evening hours.

Challenge: Your loved one becomes increasingly anxious and confused as evening approaches, pacing restlessly and repeatedly asking to "go home" even though you're already there. The behavior disrupts dinner time and bedtime routines, leaving you both exhausted and stressed.

Solution: Create a structured, calming evening routine that begins before sunset. Use environmental cues like adjusting lighting, playing soothing music, and engaging in quiet activities to help ease the transition from day to night. Recognize that your loved one's anxiety is real to them, and respond with gentle reassurance rather than correction.

Example: Starting at 4:00 PM each day, begin dimming some lights while keeping others bright enough to prevent shadows. Put on your loved one's favorite music softly in the background, and involve them in a simple activity like folding towels together or looking through a familiar photo album. When they express anxiety about "going home," instead of explaining that they are home, try saying something like, "I can see you're feeling worried. Let's sit together in your favorite chair and look at these family pictures while we have a cup of tea." This routine helps create a sense of security and calm during a challenging time of day.

Practical tips for managing sundowning:

1. Establish a consistent, calming evening routine.

2. Develop evening playlists to signal the end of the day.

3. Manage light exposure by ensuring the home environment is well-lit, gradually transitioning to softer, warmer lighting as the evening progresses.

4. Minimize shadows and visual confusion by closing curtains or blinds, and create a soothing atmosphere with familiar and comforting objects.

5. Redirect restless energy with gentle walks, simple sorting tasks, or other engaging activities that provide a sense of accomplishment.

6. Offer reassurance and comfort through gentle touch, soothing words, and moments of quiet togetherness, recognizing the power of human connection.

7. Prioritize self-care for care partners by seeking support, engaging in restorative activities, and maintaining emotional and physical well-being.

8. Approach sundowning with patience, flexibility, and creative problem-solving, adapting strategies as needed to meet the needs of each individual.

9. Draw strength and guidance from faith, trusting in God's constant presence and protection, and allowing divine wisdom to guide actions and attitudes in moments of challenge.

In every gentle touch, every soothing word, and every shared moment of peace, you honor the immeasurable worth of those you serve, bearing witness to the unshakable truth that love has the power to illuminate even the darkest of nights. Remember that God is your constant source of strength, shelter, and guidance as you navigate the challenges of sundowning. Trust in His unfailing love and let His truth be your shield, bringing light and hope to every evening.

Chapter 29: Exploring Alternative Therapies

Scripture: "Pleasant words are as an honeycomb, sweet to the soul, and health to the bones." (Proverbs 16:24, KJV)

God's wisdom reminds us that words of kindness and comfort can bring deep healing to the body and spirit. As we explore alternative therapies, we seek approaches that offer this same sweetness and nourishment to those in our care.

Devotional: In the journey of caregiving, God opens doors to various paths of healing and connection. Through His guidance, we discover therapeutic approaches can take many forms, each offering unique blessings. As we seek ways to complement traditional care, God grants us discernment to explore different methods that nurture the whole person—body, mind, and spirit. He leads us to therapies that bring comfort, joy, and a sense of sacred connection. When we approach alternative therapies with open hearts and minds, God's wisdom guides our choices, helping us find approaches that promote deep well-being. Trust that as you explore these diverse paths of care, God's healing presence flows through each one, offering fresh possibilities for restoration and relationship.

Prayer: *Loving God, guide me as I explore alternative therapies to complement the care I provide. Grant me discernment to choose approaches that align with Your healing wisdom. Open my heart to* *new experiences that may bring comfort, joy, and a deeper sense of connection to my loved one. Help me create a sacred space for these therapeutic encounters, where Your presence can be felt and experienced. When I feel uncertain or overwhelmed in this exploration, remind me of Your constant guidance and the value of seeking out new avenues of care. May each alternative therapy I incorporate become a channel of Your love and grace, nourishing the body, mind, and spirit. Thank You for the many paths of healing You provide and for the opportunity to discover them together. Amen.*

Introducing alternative therapies into your care routine can provide fresh perspectives and valuable tools for supporting your loved one. These approaches offer opportunities for meaningful engagement and can sometimes ease the challenges of daily care.

Exploring therapies like music, art, aromatherapy, or pet therapy may reveal new ways to connect with your loved one. You might find that a particular scent helps calm agitation, or that creating art together fosters a sense of accomplishment and joy for each of you.

As you introduce new therapies, observe how your loved one responds. Their reactions, even if subtle, can guide you in tailoring activities to their preferences and needs. Stay open to adjusting your approach, and don't hesitate to consult with healthcare providers about integrating these therapies into your overall care plan.

Together, you can find activities that resonate with your shared interests and individual needs. Whether it's swaying to favorite tunes in music therapy, creating a colorful masterpiece in art therapy, or enjoying the soothing presence of a therapy animal, these experiences can foster moments of joy and relaxation.

Consider creating a "therapy toolkit" together, filled with items that engage different senses—perhaps a playlist of beloved songs, aromatic oils, or tactile objects for art projects. Having these resources readily available can help during times of stress or when you're looking for a shared activity.

As you explore these therapies, focus on the process rather than the outcome. The true value lies in the moments of engagement, expression, and connection they provide. Celebrate the small victories—a smile during a music session, a moment of calm after aromatherapy, or a shared laugh during pet therapy.

By embracing alternative therapies, you're opening doors to new forms of communication, expression, and well-being. These shared experiences can strengthen your bond, providing fresh ways to connect and find meaning together. Let these creative approaches be a source of light, offering moments of joy, peace, and connection in your daily life.

Challenge: Feeling overwhelmed by the many alternative therapy options available and unsure how to begin incorporating them into your daily caregiving routine without it feeling forced or overwhelming for your loved one.

Solution: Start with simple, natural therapeutic activities that feel like a natural extension of daily life. Choose one approach that aligns with your loved one's interests and preferences, introducing it gradually as part of your regular routine.

Example: Noticing your loved one becomes agitated in the afternoons, you decide to explore music therapy. Instead of formally announcing "it's time for music therapy," you play their favorite songs softly during lunch. When you notice this brings calm, you expand by creating different playlists for different times of day. This gradual integration of music creates a therapeutic environment without feeling clinical, and you notice your loved one humming along and seeming more relaxed during previously difficult transition times.

Tips for Incorporating Alternative Therapies:

1. Start with one therapy at a time, based on your loved one's interests and needs. Consult with healthcare providers for guidance.

2. Introduce alternative therapies gradually and in a familiar, comfortable environment. Start with short sessions and simple activities.

3. Look for ways to integrate therapies into daily activities. Many alternative therapies can be adapted to fit into regular routines.

4. Focus on creating a relaxed, no-pressure environment. Emphasize enjoyment over achievement.

5. Approach alternative therapies with realistic expectations. The effects may be subtle and vary from day to day.

6. Always consult with healthcare providers before introducing new therapies, especially if they involve physical activity or the use of essential oils.

7. Pay attention to responses and adjust accordingly. Be prepared to modify activities based on changing needs and preferences.

8. Remember that the relational aspect of these therapies is often as important as the activities themselves. Focus on fostering connection and comfort.

As you explore the rich world of alternative therapies, may you find approaches that bring sweetness to the soul and health to the body. Trust that God is guiding you in this exploration, leading you to therapies that will nourish and uplift in deeply meaningful ways. Embrace the journey with curiosity and grace, knowing that each step holds the potential for new discoveries and blessings.

Chapter 30: Navigating Family Dynamics

Scripture: "Behold, how good and how pleasant it is for brethren to dwell together in unity!" (Psalm 133:1, KJV)

God's heart for families is one of unity and mutual support. As we navigate the complexities of family caregiving, He invites us to embrace this vision of togetherness, even amidst the challenges.

Devotional: God provides the wisdom and grace needed to navigate relationships with love. Through His guidance, we discover ways to honor individual differences while maintaining a shared commitment to our loved one's well-being. God gives us the patience to listen, the empathy to understand, and the creativity to find solutions that work for everyone. When family dynamics become strained, He reminds us that unity is not about perfection, but about a willingness to keep showing up for each other. As we seek God's perspective, He helps us see the value in each family member's contributions, and the strength that comes from supporting one another. Trust that as you lean on God's wisdom, He will guide your family to a place of greater understanding, compassion, and collaboration in this caregiving journey.

Prayer: *God, I come to You seeking guidance and grace as I navigate the complexities of family caregiving. When disagreements arise or tensions run high, help me remain rooted in Your love and to* *approach each interaction with a spirit of understanding. Grant me the wisdom to communicate clearly, the patience to listen deeply, and the courage to have tough conversations when needed. Help me see each family member through Your eyes, recognizing the unique gifts and perspectives they bring. In the face of division, bring unity. Where there is hurt, bring healing. Where there is uncertainty, bring wisdom. May our family grow stronger and more compassionate as we learn to care for each other while caring for our loved one. Thank You for being the glue that holds us together. Amen.*

As a primary caregiver, you're often at the center of family dynamics surrounding care. Navigating these relationships while focusing on your loved one's needs can be challenging and emotionally taxing.

Recognize that family members may have different ways of coping with and contributing to care. Some might dive into hands-on assistance, while others may offer support from a distance. Try to approach these differences with understanding, acknowledging that each person's capacity to help may vary.

Open communication is key. Regular family meetings or updates can help keep everyone informed and involved. Be clear about your loved one's needs and your own limitations. Don't be afraid to ask for specific help or to delegate tasks. And remember that it's important to set boundaries and limits to protect yourself and your loved one. For example, some in your family may give unsolicited advice, even if they don't really understand the nature of dementia. Learn how to say "Thank you. I appreciate you're saying this because you care and want to help. It would really help if you would read this brochure that helped me understand the process people go through with the changes of dementia. I could also use help with …" Or a family member may begin to argue with the loved one with dementia when he or she is confused. Take them aside and let them know that you have found it isn't helpful and only further agitates and confuses the person, and share what you have learned about meeting that person in their own reality.

Recognize that each family member, including the person with cognitive changes, brings unique perspectives and strengths to the situation. Creating an environment where everyone feels heard and valued can lead to more effective care and stronger family bonds.

Consider establishing regular family check-ins or activities that involve multiple family members. This could be as simple as shared meals, video calls with distant relatives, or collaborative decision-making about care plans. These interactions can help maintain connections and ensure that everyone feels included.

Be patient with one another as you all adjust to new roles and dynamics. Misunderstandings may occur, but approaching conflicts with empathy and a willingness to find common ground can lead to resolutions that benefit everyone.

Challenge: Feeling frustrated and overwhelmed when family members offer well-meaning but uninformed advice about your loved one's care, or criticize your caregiving decisions without understanding the daily realities of dementia care.

Solution: Create structured ways to educate family members about dementia while also giving them specific, meaningful ways to contribute to care. Use regular family meetings to share updates, educational resources, and delegate tasks based on each person's abilities and availability.

Example: Your sister frequently suggests that Mom "just needs to try harder" to remember things and questions your decision to provide simple, structured routines. Instead of becoming defensive, you invite her to join you for a care planning meeting with Mom's doctor. After the appointment, you share a specific dementia care guide and say, "I know you want what's best for Mom. Would you be willing to take her to lunch every Tuesday? It would give her something to look forward to, and you could see firsthand how her needs change throughout the day. It would also give me time to attend my support group." This approach helps your sister better understand Mom's condition while giving her a meaningful way to contribute to care.

Tips for Navigating Family Dynamics:

1. Communicate openly and honestly about each family member's abilities and limitations in providing care.

2. Establish regular family meetings to share updates, discuss concerns, and make collective decisions.

3. Use "I" statements and active listening to foster understanding and minimize conflict.

4. Focus on your loved one's needs and well-being when making care decisions, rather than personal agendas.

5. Be willing to compromise and adapt roles and responsibilities as needed.

6. Create a supportive environment where each family member feels heard and validated.

7. Seek outside support, such as family therapy or support groups, to deal with complex emotions.

8. Celebrate moments of connection as a family.

9. Make time for family activities outside of the caregiving context to nurture relationships.

10. Approach challenges with patience, empathy, and a commitment to working together.

11. Share brochures and information about what you have learned about dementia.

Remember, the dementia care journey is one that no family chooses, but it is a path that many find themselves navigating together. Amid the challenges and uncertainties, there is also an opportunity for families to deepen their connections, to learn from each other, and to discover reserves of strength and resilience they never knew they had. Trust that as you seek God's wisdom and guidance, He will equip your family to face each step of this journey with grace, compassion, and unity.

Chapter 31: Addressing Challenging Behaviors with Compassion

Scripture: "Put on therefore, as the elect of God, holy and beloved, bowels of mercies, kindness, humbleness of mind, meekness, longsuffering." (Colossians 3:12, KJV)

As God's chosen ones, we are called to clothe ourselves with compassion, kindness, humility, gentleness, and patience. These qualities are essential as we navigate the challenges of caregiving, especially when faced with difficult behaviors.

Devotional: In moments of challenging behaviors, God invites us to draw from the well of His compassion. He reminds us we are His beloved children, equipped with the capacity for mercy, kindness, and patience that goes beyond our own strength. As we seek to understand the needs and emotions behind our loved one's actions, God grants us the humility to look past the surface and respond with gentleness. When our own patience feels stretched thin, we can lean into the limitless reservoir of God's grace, trusting that He will provide the wisdom and strength we need for each moment.

Every challenging behavior is an opportunity to extend the same compassion and long-suffering that God has shown to us.

Prayer: *God, grant me the grace to look beyond the surface of my loved one's actions and to respond with understanding and mercy. In moments when my patience feels depleted, renew my spirit with Your* *enduring compassion. Help me create an atmosphere of peace and security, where even the most difficult moments can be met with Your calming presence. Thank You for equipping me with all I need to face each challenge with Your heart of compassion. Amen.*

Facing challenging behaviors can be one of the most difficult aspects of caregiving. Your loved one is not acting out intentionally, but is often trying to communicate a need or feeling they can't express in other ways.

When confronted with challenging behaviors, take a deep breath and center yourself. Your calm presence can be a powerful tool in de-escalating tense situations. Use a gentle tone of voice and, if appropriate, offer a comforting touch. These simple actions can convey safety and reassurance.

Try to look beyond the behavior to understand what might be triggering it. Is your loved one hungry, tired, or in pain? Are they overstimulated by their environment? By addressing the underlying need, you can often ease the distressing behavior.

Together, try to identify patterns or triggers that lead to challenging behaviors. This might involve keeping a simple log of when difficulties arise and what was happening before them. By recognizing these patterns, you can work together to avoid or modify situations that cause distress.

Sometimes, simply being present and offering reassurance can be more powerful than any specific intervention. Your love and dedication are the most valuable gifts you can offer during these challenging moments.

Challenge: You become increasingly frustrated and emotionally drained when your loved one exhibits repetitive behaviors, like constantly asking about going home or accusing you of taking their belongings, making it difficult to maintain a compassionate response.

Solution: Develop a "compassion pause" practice where you take a moment to remind yourself that these behaviors stem from the disease, not defiance. Create a mental checklist to help you identify possible unmet needs behind the behavior before responding, and keep a collection of go-to gentle responses ready for common situations.

Example: When your loved one repeatedly accuses you of stealing their wallet (which they actually placed in a drawer last week), instead of defending yourself or arguing, pause and take a deep breath. Acknowledge their feelings by saying something like, "I see you're worried about your wallet. That must feel scary. Would you like me to help you look for it?" After finding it together, redirect them to a calming activity you both enjoy. This compassionate approach helps them feel heard and supported rather than dismissed, often reducing their anxiety and the frequency of accusations.

Tips for Responding to Challenging Behaviors with Compassion:

1. Take a deep breath and pause before reacting. This moment of mindfulness can help you respond with intention and patience.

2. Look for the emotions and needs behind the behavior. Is your loved one feeling scared, overwhelmed, or in pain?

3. Speak in a calm, soothing voice, even if you're feeling frustrated or tired. Your tone can help de-escalate tense situations.

4. Offer a gentle touch or hug if appropriate. Physical touch can be a powerful way to communicate love and reassurance.

5. Validate your loved one's feelings, even if you don't agree with their perspective. Acknowledgment can help them feel heard and understood.

6. Try redirecting their attention to a favorite activity or hobby that brings them joy and comfort.

7. Ensure their basic needs for sleep, nutrition, hydration, and pain management are being met consistently.

8. Create a calm, peaceful environment with minimal noise and distractions.

9. Take care of yourself and prioritize your own self-care. Accepting help and taking breaks can prevent burnout and enable you to be a more compassionate care partner.

Trust that God is with you in every challenging moment, providing the strength, wisdom, and grace you need to respond with His heart. Your consistent compassion, even in the face of difficulty, is a powerful testament to the enduring nature of your love and God's faithfulness.

SPIRITUAL AND PERSONAL GROWTH

Chapter 32: Nurturing Your Own Faith as a Care Partner

Scripture: "What time I am afraid, I will trust in thee." (Psalm 56:3, KJV)

When faced with the challenges and uncertainties of caregiving, we can find comfort and strength in God's unwavering presence and love.

Devotional: As a care partner, you pour so much of yourself into supporting your loved one. It's easy to become physically and spiritually drained. But God understands the demands of your role and wants to be your source of strength and renewal. He invites you to bring your fears, your weariness, and your doubts to Him, trusting in His faithfulness to sustain you. When you feel overwhelmed, remember that God is your refuge and your ever-present help. He delights in the moments you spend in His presence, no matter how brief or imperfect they may seem. As you make space for prayer, reading scripture, and quiet reflection, God will fill you with His peace and grace, equipping you to continue loving and serving with a heart anchored in His strength.

Prayer: *God, thank You for being my constant source of strength and comfort as I navigate the joys and challenges of caregiving. When I feel tired or discouraged, remind me to turn to You, trusting in Your promise to renew my spirit. Help me carve out moments in my day to connect with You, even if it's* *just a whispered prayer or a few verses of scripture. As I spend time in Your presence, fill me with Your peace, Your wisdom, and Your compassion. Give me the faith to trust You in all circumstances, knowing that You are always by my side. Thank You for the privilege of caring for my loved one. May my life and my service be a reflection of Your unfailing love. Amen.*

Your dedication, love, and tireless efforts have not gone unnoticed. Your role is challenging, often thankless, but profoundly important. It's okay to have hard days and to feel overloaded at times. But in those moments, remember that you can lean on God's strength and find rest in His loving arms.

It's essential to nurture your own faith while supporting your loved one. Trusting in God's presence and finding strength in your faith can help you navigate the challenges and uncertainties of your caregiving journey. Remember that you're never alone, and that God is with you every step of the way.

Maintaining a strong connection to your faith can provide you with the comfort, guidance, and strength you need as a care partner. Engage in practices that bring you closer to God and help you find peace amid the challenges. Attend church services or spiritual group meetings regularly, as they can offer a sense of community, support, and shared faith. If you find it difficult to attend in person, consider joining online services or prayer groups.

Make time for personal devotion and reflection. Read scriptures that resonate with you and meditate on their messages of hope, love, and resilience. Pray for guidance, strength, and wisdom, and trust that God is listening and caring for you. Find comfort knowing you're fulfilling a sacred mission by caring for your loved one.

Practice gratitude by acknowledging the blessings in your life, even amid hardship. Share your blessings and your challenges with trusted friends, family members, or fellow care partners who understand your situation. Seek their support and prayers when you feel overwhelmed and be open to receiving the help and encouragement they offer.

> **Challenge:** Feeling overwhelmed or burnt out and struggling to find time and energy for your own spiritual needs.
>
> **Solution:** Prioritize your faith as a vital part of your self-care routine. Set aside dedicated time for prayer, reflection, and spiritual nourishment, even if it's just a few minutes each day. Reach out to your faith community for support and guidance when you need it.
>
> **Example:** Create a daily ritual of reading a favorite scripture passage or devotional, followed by a few moments of quiet prayer or meditation. This simple practice can help you stay centered and connected to your faith, even on the most challenging days.

Remember that your faith is a source of hope and strength, not just for your loved one, but for yourself as well. Embrace the peace and comfort that comes from trusting in God's plan, even when the path ahead seems uncertain. Know that each day brings new opportunities for joy, growth, and connection with your loved one and with your faith. As you continue to nurture your own spiritual well-being, you'll find the resilience and grace needed to love and serve with a heart rooted in God's unfailing love.

Chapter 33: Maintaining Dignity

Scripture: "But by the grace of God I am what I am: and his grace which was bestowed upon me was not in vain." (1 Corinthians 15:10, KJV)

God's grace reminds us that every person is inherently valuable, regardless of their abilities or circumstances. As caregivers, we have the privilege of reflecting this truth through our actions and interactions.

Devotional: God sees the inherent worth in every person He creates. As we care for our loved ones, He guides us in upholding their dignity, even as their needs change. Through His wisdom, we learn to show respect and honor, even when providing extensive assistance. God understands the delicate balance between offering help and promoting independence, and He equips us with the discernment to find that balance. As we seek His guidance, He enables us to protect our loved one's sense of self-worth while meeting their practical needs. When we care with respect and compassion, we reflect God's love and affirm the value He places on every individual. Trust that God is with you, teaching you to provide care that preserves dignity and mirrors His heart for your loved one.

Prayer: *God, guide me in providing care that upholds my loved one's dignity. When I must assist with personal tasks, show me how to do so with respect and sensitivity. Help me honor their choices and preferences, while also ensuring their safety and* *well-being. In moments when I must decide on their behalf, remind me of their inherent worth in Your eyes. Grant me the wisdom to encourage their independence whenever possible, and the compassion to offer support with gentleness and respect. May my actions and words always affirm their value and reflect Your love. Thank You for entrusting me with the sacred task of caregiving. Amen.*

You play a crucial role in maintaining your loved one's sense of dignity and autonomy. By involving them in decisions and respecting their choices, you affirm their value and personhood. This approach requires patience, creativity, and commitment.

You may find yourself balancing safety concerns with the desire to promote independence. Look for opportunities to offer choices, even if they seem small. Simple options like "Would you like to wear the blue shirt or the green one?" can provide a sense of control and self-expression.

When assistance is necessary, strive to provide it discreetly and respectfully. Always speak to your loved one as an adult, avoiding infantilizing language. Your tone and manner of interaction can significantly impact their sense of dignity and self-worth.

Encouraging independence in safe activities not only preserves dignity but can also help maintain skills and boost confidence. Be mindful of the fine line between necessary help and unintentional over-assistance. Your supportive presence, ready to help when needed, can provide reassurance without overshadowing their capabilities.

Challenge: Feeling the urge to take over tasks or make decisions for your loved one, even when they are still capable of participating.

Solution: Pause and ask yourself, "Is there a way to involve my loved one in this task or decision, even if it's just a small part?" Look for opportunities to offer choices and encourage independence while providing support as needed.

Example: If you notice your loved one struggling to button their shirt, your first instinct may be to do it for them. Instead, remember the importance of maintaining their dignity. Try asking, "Would you like me to help with the top buttons or the bottom buttons?" This gives them a sense of control and allows them to participate in the process, even as you provide assistance.

Tips for Honoring Your Loved One:

1. Involve your loved one in decision-making whenever possible, no matter how small the choices may seem.

2. Encourage independence in safe activities, even if it takes more time or the result isn't perfect.

3. When assistance becomes necessary, provide it with gentleness and respect. Use collaborative language that acknowledges their autonomy.

4. Limit options to two or three when presenting choices to avoid overwhelming your loved one.

5. Recognize that changes in your loved one's abilities can be emotionally challenging for each of you. Be gentle with yourself and seek support.

6. Cultivate a sense of presence and connection when assisting your loved one with daily tasks, infusing the moment with tenderness and respect.

7. Draw strength from the knowledge that your loved one's inherent dignity and value remain unchanged, regardless of cognitive decline.

In honoring the dignity of your loved one, you affirm the very essence of your shared humanity, forever bound by the unbreakable ties of love and compassion. Remember that God's grace is sufficient to guide and sustain you as you provide care that upholds the sacred worth of your loved one.

Chapter 34: Maintaining Social Connections

Scripture: "And let us consider one another to provoke unto love and to good works: Not forsaking the assembling of ourselves together, as the manner of some is; but exhorting one another: and so much the more, as ye see the day approaching." (Hebrews 10:24-25, KJV)

God created us for community and connection, providing opportunities to maintain and nurture relationships that strengthen us, reflecting His design for mutual support and encouragement. You'll notice that the theme of social connections appears throughout several chapters of this devotional. This repetition is intentional, because your well-being and that of your loved one depend so deeply on staying connected to others.

Devotional: God gives us ways to stay connected even when it feels challenging, knowing that relationships sustains you both. He understands when maintaining connections is difficult and helps us find creative solutions to stay in community. As we prioritize nurturing relationships, God's love flows through these connections, providing strength and support. Trust that He guides your efforts to build networks of care and understanding. Remember that in maintaining social bonds, God's presence becomes tangible through the love and encouragement of others.

Prayer: *God, guide me in nurturing important relationships while caregiving. When isolation threatens, help me find ways to stay connected. Grant me wisdom to build and maintain supportive relationships. Remind me I'm surrounded by Your family, ready to offer care and support. Help me create opportunities for meaningful social connection, and keep my heart open to receiving the love and encouragement of others. When caregiving demands feel too much, give me the grace and courage to reach out. May these connections be a source of strength for my loved one and myself. Thank You for the gift of community. Amen.*

While caregiving responsibilities may challenge social ties, even small moments of connection matter deeply. Approaching relationships with creativity and openness helps build sustaining supportive communities.

As you learned in earlier chapters, regular interactions with friends, family, or support groups can provide you with emotional support, practical advice, and much-needed respite.

Maintaining social ties might require creativity and adaptability but the effort is worthwhile. Each genuine moment of connection, no matter how brief or simple, has value. Whether it's a visit from a friend, participating in a community event, or joining a support group, these interactions can boost mood, provide a sense of belonging, and even help maintain cognitive function.

It's important to recognize that connections come in many forms, and that quality often matters more than quantity. A single heartfelt conversation or shared moment of laughter can be more nourishing than hours of superficial interaction.

Shared activities are a powerful way to nurture social bonds. Engaging in hobbies with others can boost self-esteem and create joyful interaction. Care partners also benefit from shared experiences with their loved one and their own support network. Regular outings or visits, even if brief, provide much-needed respite and remind care partners they are not alone.

Learning to communicate openly about the diagnosis is another key aspect of maintaining social ties. Many people, even close friends and family, may feel unsure about how to interact with someone living with dementia. As a care partner, you can bridge this gap by educating others about the condition, its progression, and how best to offer support. By discussing the topic honestly, you can break down stigma, foster understanding, and create a network of support that extends beyond immediate family.

> **Challenge:** Feeling overwhelmed by caregiving responsibilities, leading to social isolation.
>
> **Solution:** Set specific, achievable goals for social interaction and ask for help in meeting them. This might mean arranging for respite care so you can attend a weekly coffee date with friends or asking a family member to sit with your loved one for an hour so you can go for a walk with a neighbor.

Example: You know you need social connection to avoid burnout, but feel guilty leaving your loved one alone. Try asking a friend or family member to come sit with your loved one for just 30 minutes once a week so you can video chat with your best friend. It's a small step but it's a start in honoring your own needs.

Tips for Nurturing Social Ties:

1. Prioritize relationships that bring comfort and joy. Focus on the connections that are most meaningful and supportive for you and your loved one. Quality of interaction is more important than quantity, so invest in the relationships that truly nourish each of you.

2. Be open to new forms of social engagement. As symptoms progress, traditional forms of socializing may become challenging. Embrace creativity and flexibility to explore new ways of connecting that bring joy and a sense of togetherness.

3. Set aside dedicated time for your own social needs. Care partners, it's crucial to nurture your own social well-being, even amidst the demands of caregiving. Set specific, achievable goals for social interaction each week, whether it's a phone call with a friend, a support group meeting, or a shared hobby with a family member. Honoring your need for connection will help sustain you emotionally and spiritually.

4. Engage in shared activities to bond and create joyful moments. Participating in hobbies and activities together can foster a sense of connection and shared enjoyment. This might mean working on a simple puzzle, listening to favorite music, or going for a nature walk. For care partners, shared experiences provide respite, normalcy, and the reminder that you're not alone.

5. Adapt communication and interaction to changing needs. As memory changes progress, the nature of social interactions may shift. Verbal communication may become less central, while physical affection, visual cues, and emotional attunement take on new importance. By meeting your loved one where they are and finding new ways to express care and understanding, you can continue to nurture a deep sense of connection.

6. Educate others to foster understanding and support. Many people feel uncertain about how to interact with someone living with dementia. As a care partner, you can bridge this gap by openly discussing the condition, its progression, and how others can best offer support. By providing guidance and reassurance, you can help create a wider network of informed, compassionate allies.

7. Create space for interactions that aren't focused on the disease. While openly discussing the diagnosis is important, it's equally vital to create opportunities for your loved one and yourself to

simply be yourselves. Engage in conversations and activities that center on your interests, memories, and the joys of the present moment. These interactions affirm your multi-faceted identities and provide a sense of normalcy and respite.

8. Connect with others who are on a similar path. Joining support groups, either in-person or online, can provide invaluable emotional support, practical advice, and a sense of belonging. Sharing experiences and learning from others who understand the challenges and joys of this journey can be incredibly uplifting and empowering.

Every effort to stay connected matters—whether it's a brief phone call, a shared prayer, or a moment of laughter with a friend. God has placed people in your life to walk alongside you and He understands when maintaining these connections feels challenging. Trust that He will guide you to the right people and opportunities for meaningful connection, even as your caregiving responsibilities evolve. You don't have to navigate this path alone. Each time you reach out, each relationship you nurture, and each moment of connection you create honors your needs and God's design for community. May you find strength, comfort, and renewed purpose through the precious gift of relationships He provides.

Thank you for allowing me to be part of your caregiving journey. I hope this devotional has provided comfort, guidance, and encouragement. While this short guide focuses on the spiritual aspects of caregiving, I'd like to share another resource that approaches caregiving through a different lens. My novel, "The Nurse," while fiction, is a heartfelt love story that follows a caregiver's journey. It was inspired by my short film of the same name which you can watch by scanning the QR code below.

The story weaves together themes of love, dedication, and the deep bonds that form through caregiving.

Whether through this devotional, the film, or the novel, my hope is to honor and support caregivers like you who give so much of themselves in service to others.

You can find "The Nurse" novel on Amazon: https://a.co/d/bXqaTZn

Short Film

With gratitude and appreciation,

Joyce Kostakis

Printed in Great Britain
by Amazon

59216041R00099